LEAVES

LEAVES

The formation, characteristics and uses of hundreds of leaves found in all parts of the world

❧ ❧ ❧ ❧ ❧ ❧ ❧ ❧ ❧ ❧ ❧ ❧

photographs by

KJELL B. SANDVED

National Museum of Natural History,

Smithsonian Institution, Washington, D.C.

text by

885

GHILLEAN TOLMIE PRANCE

Senior Vice-President for Science, The New York Botanical Garden

CROWN PUBLISHERS, INC. ❧ NEW YORK

This book is dedicated

to

DR. PORTER M. KIER,

enthusiastic naturalist, former Director

of the National Museum of Natural History,

The Smithsonian Institution

All photographs in this book are by Kjell Sandved except the photographs that appear on the following pages, which are by Ghillean T. Prance: pages 35; 40, right; 41, both; 53, lower left; 69; 73, top left; 77, bottom left; 84, upper right; 88, lower left and right; 89, upper left, lower left; 92, both; 95; 96; 97; 110, all; 114, lower left, upper right; 115, right; 116, top left, middle and lower right; 119; 120; 128, both; 144; 149, bottom; 151, top left; 154, top right; 161, top; 168–169; 170–171; 172; 194, bottom right; 200; 201; 202, both; 203, right; 204–205; 206; 207; 208. The photo on page 82 is by Scott A. Mori.

Grateful acknowledgment is hereby made to Paul Simon Music

for permission to reprint from *Leaves That Are Green* by Paul

Simon copyright © 1965 by Paul Simon. All rights reserved.

Published by Crown Publishers, Inc.,

One Park Avenue, New York, New York 10016

and Printed simultaneously in Canada by General Publishing Company Limited

Manufactured in Japan

Library of Congress Cataloging in Publication Data

Prance, Ghillean T., 1937–

Leaves, the formation, characteristics, and uses

of hundreds of leaves found in all parts of the world.

Includes index.

1. Leaves.   I. Sandved, Kjell Bloch, date.

II. Title.

QK649.P7 1984   582'.01   83-14336

ISBN: 0-517-551527

Book design by Camilla Filancia

10 9 8 7 6 5 4 3 2 1

First Edition

CONTENTS

ACKNOWLEDGMENTS

We are grateful to Anne E. Prance for much assistance with the preparation of the manuscript, to Frances Maroncelli and Patricia Kidd for typing the several versions of this manuscript, to Bobbi Angell for preparing the line drawings, and to Don Black for producing the Scanning Electron microscope photographs of leaf hairs. The authors are grateful to The New York Botanical Garden for the opportunity to travel to many places around the world to study and photograph leaves.

GHILLEAN T. PRANCE

I am deeply grateful to my many friends among the eminent scientists in the National Museum of Natural History who through the years have stimulated my interest and corrected my errant ways in the various branches of natural history.

I am honored to have had a foremost botanist and seasoned Amazon explorer, Dr. Ghillean T. Prance, sort out from myriads of facts relevant information in a text that has lifted my venture from the plane of the aesthetics of leaves to a publication of educational value. I particularly thank my dear friend, Barbara Bedette, for her tireless help in my photography, research, and typing of manuscripts.

A special thank-you goes to:

Outside the Smithsonian Institution:

Dr. Graziela Barroso, Jardim Botânico do Rio de Janeiro
Dr. Roger Beaver, Chian Mai University, Thailand
Claudia Bonsack
Dr. Roberto Burle-Marx, Rio de Janeiro
Dr. J. Linsley Gressitt, Wau Ecology Institute, New Guinea
Dr. M. P. Harris, Galapagos Islands
Dr. Leo Hickey, Peabody Museum, Yale University
Dr. Kenneth P. Lamb, University of Papua, New Guinea
Dr. João Murça Pires, IPEAN, Belém, Brazil
Dr. Ivan Polunin, University of Singapore
Dr. Peter Raven, Missouri Botanical Garden
Dr. Laura Schuster, Universidad de la Selva, Peru
Dr. J. S. Womersley, Lae Botanical Garden, New Guinea
Dr. Fernandez Yepez, University of Maracay, Venezuela

Of the Smithsonian Institution:

Dr. Wilton S. Dillon
Dr. Douglas C. Ferguson
Dr. Raymond Fosberg
Francis M. Greenwell
Madeleine S. Jacobs
Charlene James-Duguid
Drs. Mark and Diane Littler
Jack F. Marquardt
Dr. Robert W. Read
Dr. Mary E. Rice
Dr. Klaus Ruetzler
Dr. Curtis W. Sabrosky
Dr. Lyman Smith
Dr. Paul and Phyllis Spangler
Ted and Rose Ella Spilman
George C. Steyskal
Dr. Edward L. Todd
Dr. Thomas R. Waller

KJELL B. SANDVED

Introduction

Leaves, leaves, leaves. They are all around us. They color our world green. For each person on earth there are millions of green leaves bringing nourishment to all flesh and sustaining the oxygen level in the air we breathe. And yet we know so little about the diversity of these senior inhabitants of earth. As urban creatures, we have lost touch with nature, so much so that most of us see in a leaf only a repetition of the next one. How true it is that the common things in life are too often taken for granted and overlooked, and leaves are among them.

In the scientific literature, the leaves of plants have always taken a back seat to their flowers. In our library at the National Museum of Natural History I have found hundreds of books with special emphasis on flowers, but none with emphasis strictly on leaf diversity, uses, and color. Compared to the flower, the colorful sexual part of the plant, the leaf is "only" the more prosaic and symbolic heart and stomach of the plant; through transpiration and osmotic pressure within the cell, the leaf literally sucks water and dissolved minerals from the soil; then, with the sun's radiant energy, the leaf manufactures sugars and starches for the plant through the process of photosynthesis.

To some it would seem embarrassing, to others impressive

that the orangutan recognizes more species of plants than we do. Out of sheer necessity the orangutan ("man of the forest") must distinguish between a great number of leaves—which ones are edible and which ones are not. While photographing leaves near Sandakan in Sabah, Malaysia, I noticed how these animals are apparently testing edibility by picking leaves or breaking off twigs and letting them dangle for some time from their mouths like a cigarette before they let them drop. This they do even during play and social interaction. During the coevolution of plants and animals, the constant feeding on leaves by insects and mammals provided the pressure for the development of chemical defenses in the leaves of many of the 330,000 existing plants today.

Diversity and variation is an intrinsic part of the law of evolution—nature's way of ensuring success. In plants, genetic variability is found even in leaves, for no two are exactly alike. Each leaf varies slightly from others in vein patterns and margins. Since "her right hand knoweth not what her left hand hath wrought," evolution often moves effortlessly in two or more directions at the same time, toward simplicity and toward complexity. When one form of leaf works about as well as another, both develop. The variety is considerable in leaves such as saw-toothed elms and pussy willows or the lobes in maples and oaks. Needles of conifers are actually leaves, as are the tendrils of many vines. Some leaves consist of numerous leaflets; others form larger leaves. Banana leaves have parallel veins and are easily torn in high winds but are still able to function. The variability seems endless.

As man is cutting down natural forests at unprecedented rates, he often replaces them with fast-growing, commercial trees. The chemistry of the soil is changed with the irretrievable loss of some species of its natural flora and fauna.

The greatest extinction of plants has possibly occurred in the Middle East. Filming a Smithsonian Institution excavation in Jordan of early Bronze Age man near the Dead Sea, I noticed undulating horizontal lines around every little hillside. They were pathways trodden by foraging goats and camels through the ages. The only shrubs I found to photograph had leaves with long, firm spines on both surfaces for protection. Most other less-protected plants had been browsed out of existence through the millennia. With the loss of plant life comes also the loss of animals, either through scarcity of food or through the hunter, man. Hunting, killing, and uprooting of our environment in the name of necessity has been a normal, seemingly unavoidable genetic expression of man's once "manifest destiny."

Even Charles Darwin in his youth became very fond of shooting. "I do not believe that anyone," he wrote, "could have shown more zeal for the most holy cause than I did for shooting birds. How well I remember killing my first snipe, and my excitement was so great that I had much difficulty in reloading my gun from the trembling of my hands." Later, reason curbed the instinct.

When I started fifteen years ago to prepare a book on leaves, I did not know it would take such a long time. Neither did I know that leaves have such a profusion or variation in vein patterns, shapes of the margins, color, and form.

My first walk along a steamy jungle path near a tributary of a tributary of the Amazon River was an experience never to be forgotten. The diversity of leaves was a delight to behold, and I fully realized that whereas on a five-acre woodland in the eastern United States one might find a dozen different species of trees, in the same area in the Amazon we might discover 200! Inside this dense, darkened forest the deep silence was broken only occasionally by the distant roar of a howler monkey. Only in an area where a giant tree had fallen could one fully enjoy the richness of species variation in plants which suddenly were burgeoning in the full sunlight in a profusion of competition. In such areas I found many a rare orchid, bromeliad, or other epiphytic plant.

Tendrils, which are modified leaves, were everywhere, tying together leaves with elongate, thin drip tips for a quicker runoff of raindrops. Once, after having photographed a treehopper on a nearby long, coiled tendril, I pulled it and to my amazement discovered that the tendril was curling clockwise as far as the middle and counterclockwise the rest of the way. Stretching the coil all the way out resulted in a straight, untwisted tendril with its maximum pull strength intact—a feature that has been used to good effect in telephone extension cords.

I noticed how *Peperomia,* a decorative houseplant with variegated green-and-white leaves, has a startlingly different growth pattern in its natural habitat, where the leaves are pressed flatly to the tree trunk, and creep straight up the moss-covered, buttressed base of the tree.

Here is how Darwin described his first encounter with the Brazilian rainforest in *The Voyage of the Beagle:*

> The day has passed delightfully. Delight itself, however, is a weak term to express the feelings of a naturalist who, for the first time, has wandered by himself in a Brazilian forest. The elegance of the grasses, the novelty of the parasitical plants, the beauty of the flowers, the glossy green of the foliage, but above all the general luxuriance of the vegetation, filled me with admiration. . . . To a person fond of natural history, such a day as this brings with it a deeper pleasure than he can ever hope to experience again.

The imperceptible movements of climbing plants so intrigued the great English naturalist that he had a hothouse built against the wall of his kitchen garden when he was nearing his seventieth year. "I long to stock it just like a schoolboy," he wrote to his fellow botanist Joseph Hooker. Darwin had written a book on movement in plants, and when Hooker later sent him specimens of the South

African stone plant *(Lithops),* Darwin wrote him: "You cannot imagine what pleasure your plants give me. . . . They do so amuse me. I have crawled to see them two or three times."

But we do not need to travel to exotic places to find exquisite leaves. At leisure in our own backyard or on a summer's day in a field we can pause and observe with a magnifying lens small delightful leaves and insects.

The fluttering movements of leaves have always intrigued man. The Roman poet Virgil wrote about the waving up and down of the heavy oak leaf that "gave tongue to the wind." Each leaf seems to have its own way of swaying, according to the flexibility of its stalk, its shape, and the way the leaf is attached. The flexible, flattened leaf stalk of the aspen allows the leaves to catch the faintest breeze, to shimmer and tremble like so many butterflies.

On many photographic safaris to South America, Indonesia, and New Guinea, I have enjoyed photographing pitcher plants which have modified their leaves to form water vessels to trap insects. The largest pitcher plant I have ever seen was found in a small, restricted habitat. At 10,000 feet on a windy mountain ridge of Kota Kina Balu, Sabah, a trough in the mountain chain between two valleys created a migratory pass for insects. Here was the ideal habitat for one species of large pitcher plant. Opening only one leaf, I found a dozen species of drowned insects and two species of living spiders. One species of crab spider had its foraging ground near the rim of the container where it hunted landing insects. Another species of spider had built its web farther down in the water jar where it captured other insects that managed to escape the crab spider.

A large number of insects and spiders build nests or retreats on leaves. One of the most exquisite examples of cooperative efforts by social insects to build their nests is afforded by the tailor ants of West Africa. Having observed some tailor ant colonies for a few days, I discovered a group leaving its leaf nest with the blind, white larvae in their mandibles and marching along the branches. Scout ants had picked out a site for a new nest. There I quickly rigged up my movie camera and filmed the way the stronger workers would pull individual leaves together by hanging onto each others' bodies, forming a bridge across the gap between one leaf and the next. Marching back and forth across this ant bridge, the tailor ants would sew the leaves together by touching the mouthparts of the larvae to the edge of the leaf, each time cementing a silken thread to the leaf. They were using the larvae as a weaver would use a shuttle! One team of these "shuttle-workers" wove on the top side, another team on the underside between the leaves to be sewn together. After an hour or so, two white silken layers had been spun, making that portion of the nest impermeable to water.

But of all the leaf and animal associations I have observed, the most remarkable has been the way moths use leaves in their struggle for survival. In Rancho Grande, Venezuela, the American explorer William Beebe's old hunting ground, I watched hour after hour how different moths would use different leaves as a place of concealment with mimicry and warning coloration. They bluff and they masquerade, posing as green leaves, half-eaten leaves, or partially eaten leaves with a reticulated wing disguise of skeletonized veins right down to the brownish borders. They pose as an inedible, dried brown leaf being caught at the lower end of a spider web. There are moths that hang down or stand on their heads all day long with white-tipped feet, mimicking the white-tipped fungoid stem of a dying leaf . . . all to avoid being eaten by birds or other predators. I photographed one moth which stands on its head during the day with its body and wings pointing straight up, modeling a brown, shriveled-up leaf. One moth has a realistically designed "spider" on each wing, another a fly, while others with black spots mimic leaves with holes, and others mimic the droppings of birds accurately, down to the glistening white runoff droplet. No other form of animal life on this earth, including the more numerous beetles, has evolved such close association with leaves in their struggle for survival as the little-known, albeit much maligned moths.

On another trip for the Smithsonian to the Colombian high-altitude páramo vegetation at 12,000 feet, I photographed a sunflowerlike member of the daisy family, *Espeletia grandiflora,* which grows like a tree. The budding leaves have a density of leaf hairs approaching that of a mammalian fur, possibly for protection against high-ultraviolet day radiation and occasional frost at night. However, I did not see the color-matching green frog on a leaf until I projected the slides later!

In the dry climate of South Africa, another plant has adapted to the extreme climate by forming a pea-sized round ball of a leaf with only a tiny slit of a closed window for the sunlight to enter and thus retain water.

This is the first leaf book of its kind; better and more extensive books on leaves will no doubt follow. Still, it is my hope that this book will in some small measure stimulate the younger generation to rally toward greater preservation of our precious natural heritage and to press for moratoriums on destroying any more of our splendid forests. It should be enough of a warning that the whooping crane, the condor, and our stately American chestnut trees are all on the brink of extinction. Each is irreplaceable and belongs also to those who will follow us. A new heaven and a new earth must come to pass before any of these least plants or creatures, once extinct, could reappear.

KJELL B. SANDVED
National Museum of Natural History
The Smithsonian Institution, Washington, D.C.

Photographing Leaves

by KJELL B. SANDVED

Today, the younger generation is leading the way, shooting its quarry with a telephoto lens instead of a gun. The nature photographer of today has become a more widely informed naturalist than the hunters of yesteryear. To discover new and interesting aspects of nature through the lens is a fascinating outdoor sport with all the excitement but none of the finality of shooting to kill. How much more value has one's own lasting, personal master shot of a living deer, bird, or a leaf on one's wall than a stuffed animal head with glassy eyes whose life was abruptly ended.

What is the most challenging decision facing a nature photographer? Camera choice? Hardly. I personally have extensive Nikon equipment, but were I to choose again, I might have a Canon, Minolta, Olympus, Pentax, or some other. Film? Partly. Kodachrome 25 or 64 ASA are the best films unless a color print is wanted, and then Kodacolor negative film gives superior color. Lenses? Yes, to a certain extent. A micro lens with 1:1 capability is excellent or a 35 mm to 80 mm zoom lens. If I want to go beyond that, I reverse the lens on a bellows or, for the ultimate in sharpness for tiny leaves, I use a Zeiss Luminar macro lens which I have adapted with a double release cable for shooting handheld in the field with electronic flash. Sophisticated equipment? No. The common trap that many a buyer of new equipment falls into is the belief that superior photographs will flow automatically from superior equipment. Not so. The most important element is the person behind the camera; then come a steady hand and technicalities.

Anyone can take good photographs if a few basic rules are understood and followed. The photographer is locked into the laws of optics, which are superficially rather simple. The better they are understood, the easier it is for the photographer to follow them or to break, bend, and modify them to suit his purposes.

For instance, in portrait photography we take for granted that the way we apply the lighting contributes essentially to bringing out the character of a person or establishing a mood. So it is with photographing leaves in nature. The seemingly simple design elements found in leaves present all the basic challenges in nature photography. To learn how the light influences the image, observe various leaves intermittently under changing light conditions: front lit, top lit, side lit, back lit, harshly lit by clear noon sun, softly lit and diffused by clouds, under polarized light, and with different backgrounds. Such observations can truly teach us all the art of visualizing: *seeing with the mind's eye.*

The best method for photographing leaves I can suggest is one of simplicity, and I cannot suggest it strongly enough. I call it the swivel-chair method. Bring a tripod and if possible a swivel chair into a field where you can find a great variety of leaves. Put a leaf in a vial on the tripod and observe its fine details under a magnifying glass as you turn it in relation to the sun. Or hold the leaf up to the sun as you swivel in the chair. You will be amazed to find that a full 360-degree turn gives you many different examples of the changing characteristics in the leaf. The veinlets may go from black to gray or green and then to white as the light changes and as you rotate the leaf. Observe with your mind's eye how the character and color of the leaf changes, and you will eventually be able to separate the visual impact of the various design elements of the leaf and its surrounding background.

To illustrate this simple but important point clearly, take a black pen into a darkened room with a bare bulb at a distance. As you turn the pen slowly at different angles you see the reflective white line only at certain angles to the light source. This is precisely what happens in the veins and veinlets of leaves. It is also the reason that a photograph of a spider web in clear sunlight or with electronic flash may hardly turn out at all, except when you diffuse the light or change the angle.

The visually most prominent design elements in leaves are line, form, texture, color, and space. The importance of each element varies with the amount of emphasis you want to put on one or more elements.

The *lines* in leaves are by far the most characteristic and varied element and often the least appreciated. No design element can impart a stronger attention-compelling mood setting or feature than the line.

Commonly we find curved outlines, straight central venation, transitional diagonal lines, finely reticulated lines, zigzag lines, radial or spiraling lines. Lines all contribute to a certain mood, each demanding different lighting. For example, a semicircularly curved leaf has an equal change in direction, like that of the Roman arch, imparting solidity, and may become a visual bore. A parabolically or logarithmically curved leaf has an unequal change in direction, like that of the Gothic curve, imparting elegance or lofty exultation to the leaf. A line can be subtle or it can be dominant, or you may agree at times with the bold, impressionistic statement that the line does not exist in nature; it may be nonexistent in the form of a leaf's subtle outline.

The photographic rendition of the sculptured *form* or shape of the leaf is utterly dependent on the angle and diffusion of the incoming light. Direct light from a clear sky or from a strobe light will impart harshness and contrast to a leaf. Thus a wide light source such as a large reflector, diffuser, or light overcast sky will tend to impart softness and roundness to the shape of a leaf.

Front light totally eliminates the form as well as any possible texture of the leaf. The image becomes two-dimensional. Therefore, when photographing leaves, one should never have the strobe light directly attached to the camera, but well out to the side and with a diffuser to soften the shadows.

Texture in a leaf is not only visual but also tactile, as we perceive it, for instance in leaf hairs, both by sight and by touch.

The texture of a leaf has an even greater critical dependence on the angle of the incoming light than does its form. However, it is less dependent on the size of the light source. In this way, texture and form are actually interrelated extremes of the same visual perception; texture is in the micro dimension what sculptured form is in the macro. Both are utterly dependent on side or top light and to a lesser degree on the size of the light source.

We often think of leaves as simply being an unchanging green color. But notice in early spring how many leaves follow a *color* sequence of first being vividly red or purple colored because of the initial lack of chlorophyll in the young leaves. The next color phase is yellow-green or, as in the case of evergreen leaves, dark gray-green.

The color in a leaf also varies considerably with the angle of the sun in which it is viewed, the time of day, and the weather conditions. For instance, the backlighting of a young leaf, seen in early morning light, will often result in intense yellow-green color.

Color-correcting filters in the strength of CC10R (red), CC10Y (yellow), CC10G (green), CC10C (cyan), CC10B (blue), and CC10M (magenta) can to a large degree compensate for some of the normally occurring color shifts during the day. These plastic filters can be bought at a reasonable price. They can be cut round (never touch the plastic surface, only the rim) and placed loosely in front of your lens behind the protective ultraviolet or haze glass filter.

Different light sources such as light from fluorescent and incandescent lamps, a sunset, or even rain need stronger filter compensation. Sunlight from clear sky without diffusing clouds can result in excessive contrast and harsh shadows. A thin sheet of plastic used as diffuser between the sun and the leaf will soften the shadows and help bring out the leaf's color and form.

An electronic flash is similarly a harsh light source. The light can be softened with a diffuser or with a white umbrella that broadens and diffuses the light. Diffused light can give an excellent result in closeup photography of leaves. In addition, you have the advantage of deciding the light direction: front, top, side, or back.

With top or side light a maximum of sculptured form is achieved but with less color saturation. Front light yields a maximum of color saturation but eliminates the sculptured form of the leaf. Back light reveals the fine venation. Holding the leaf up to the sun, we can trace with a magnifier every little veinlet back to the central midrib.

On a heavily overcast or rainy day, the bluish color temperature may approach 10,000 Kelvin, rendering the leaves deep blue-green. The setting sun is the least appropriate light source in which to photograph leaves. The reddish glow from the sun's color temperature is reduced to perhaps 2,000 Kelvin and renders the leaves gray-black, at times with no green at all. A color-correcting filter in the strength of CC40C (cyan) can only partially correct for the near-absent green color.

Distant forest scenes will be improved with a UV filter or haze filter and with a CC10 green color-compensating filter.

The last important design element, space, is defined as the area surrounding the leaf—in particular the background—creating a third dimension to the picture. The choice of background and its treatment greatly affects the visual impact of the leaf. When the surrounding background is wanted in sharp focus, a closed-down normal lens or a wide-angle lens is used. This creates an illusion of space but also adds a perspective distortion. When isolation of the leaf from its background is wanted, an open normal lens or a slight telephoto lens is used. This creates a narrow field of focus or sharpness, compressing the image.

These elements, singly or combined, constitute the science of seeing. Using them with forethought, anyone can learn to take good pictures of leaves.

CHAPTER 1

The Basic Functions and Structure of a Leaf

*The most wonderful thing in the world to
me is this: the leaf of a growing plant.*

LUTHER BURBANK

An autumn wind blows and down fall thousands of leaves of different sizes and shapes, red, green, orange, yellow, and brown. Each twirls and dances through the air and then settles on the ground, discarded by the tree but bearing within itself the structures of a life of usefulness and activity, a miniature chemical laboratory where life-giving and nourishing processes have taken place.

There are so many leaves on the ground of temperate countries in autumn that their removal becomes a budget item in the affairs of towns and cities. During winter we mourn the bleakness of the leafless trees, and when the first faint green haze of the nascent leaflets appears in spring our hearts lift at the sign of hope. Rarely do we stop to wonder at the miracle that these common green objects present.

The prime function of the leaf is to capture sunlight for the process of photosynthesis by which the energy for all life is made available for all the biological organisms of our planet. Photosynthesis is a complicated process by which the leaves of plants take in the carbon dioxide from the air, the roots absorb water, and, with the help of solar energy, sugar is produced. At the same time this chemical reaction produces oxygen that is released into the air. We can sum up this reaction by the following formula:

$$\text{Carbon dioxide} + \text{Water} \rightarrow \text{Glucose} + \text{Oxygen} + \text{Water}$$
$$\text{Energy}$$
$$6\,CO_2 + 12\,H_2O \rightarrow C_6H_{12}O_6 + 6\,O_2 \qquad 6\,H_2O$$

The chemical process is possible because of the presence of a green-colored substance called chlorophyll which is concentrated in minute bodies, called chloroplasts, within the leaves. The only way in which the sun's energy can be captured and turned into the sort of energy that sustains life is through this process of photosynthesis. As one would expect, such a vital process is actually a most complicated chain of chemical reactions that is still being elucidated. The biochemist Melvin Calvin was awarded the Nobel Prize for working out one of the pathways of photosynthesis. There are, however, several different ways in which the basic process of forming sugars from carbon dioxide and water is carried out within the plant kingdom. Since green plants are unique in their capacity to photosynthesize, they are the organisms upon which all other life depends for energy.

Animals do not photosynthesize and must therefore eat plants or other animals that have eaten plants to obtain their energy. Within the plants the basic glucose sugar is eventually transferred into thousands of other chemical substances such as starch, proteins, oils, and fats. The process of photosynthesis is of interest to us here because it is the basic function of a green leaf. There are also other, simpler, single-celled plants in the algae that are able to photosynthesize, but as plants become larger and more complicated they develop the organ which we call a leaf as the ideal structure for photosynthesis.

In the mid-nineteenth century German plant anatomists noted that some plants had a different type of leaf vein. In these there is a ring of large cells surrounding the veins. They also noted that the chloroplasts of these cells were different from most leaves. This was termed Kranz anatomy after its discoverer. Although details of this type of anatomy were elaborated upon over the years, it was not until ninety years later that the functional difference of these plants was discovered. They have a different biochemical pathway of photosynthesis which is much more efficient than in normal plants. This pathway was also named after its discoverers and is called the Hatch-Slack pathway or the carbon 4 pathway because of the involvement of oxalacetic acid, a C_4 acid, in this system. This much better way of fixing the sun's energy occurs only in plants with Kranz anatomy because they can collect carbon dioxide more efficiently with their sheath of specialized cells around the vascular bundles. Many members of the grass family, such as corn, sorghum, and sugarcane, have Hatch-Slack photosynthesis. It is also common in many plants of deserts and mountaintops where it is necessary for photosynthesis to occur at high temperatures and with a low water supply. This type of plant is an energy-efficient crop because it has such a good system of photosynthesis. The C_4 system accounts for the high productivity of the cornfields of the United States and of the sugarcane plantations of Brazil that are fueling many of their automobiles through transformation to alcohol.

Structure and function are closely related in all organisms. Since photosynthesis involves the capturing of light, it is logical that the basic leaf structure is thin and flat so that it exposes a considerable surface area to the light. While we still see many adaptations of plants, such as the thick, fleshy leaves of some desert plants or the leaves reduced to spines in cacti where the stem performs the photosynthesis, the basic leaf structure is a flat blade, or lamina, attached to the plant by a short stalk, called the petiole.

In order to photosynthesize, the leaf needs to obtain the water

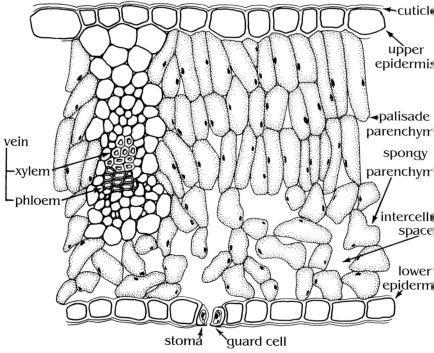

A cross-section through a typical leaf shows the different layers of tissue that occur and the technical term for each part. The stoma is seen in the epidermis of the lower surface. This section also goes through a vein which is the pipeline that transports substances in and out of the leaf. The cells of the lower part of the leaf have air spaces around the stomata which allow air to circulate for photosynthesis to take place.

BASIC FUNCTIONS AND STRUCTURE

that enters the plant through its roots and to be able to transport out the sugars and other products of photosynthesis. The petiole therefore contains vascular strands which are the pipelines that allow transport throughout the whole plant. These vascular strands, like veins, connect the central strands in the stem with the network of veins in the leaf. We can take almost any leaf and see that it has veins. It may be a series of simple parallel veins as in a grass leaf, or more commonly there is a central nerve with a network of veins crossing the leaf. These are the plumbing system through which substances move in and out of the leaves. The water from the roots is transported through the plants in elongate cells, called vessels.

The inside of the leaf is also complicated, as shown in the illustration of a section of a typical leaf. While there is much varia-

A drawing showing the structure of stomata. Different arrangements of the guard cells and the subsidiary cells next to them have led to the classification of stomata by types. The four principal types are anomocytic (A), anisocytic (B), paracytic (C), and diacytic (D). Since most groups of plants have a type of stomata characteristic to that genus or family, they are useful taxonomic characters. E and F show an open stoma, E in surface view and F in cross-section; G and H show a closed stoma from the same views.

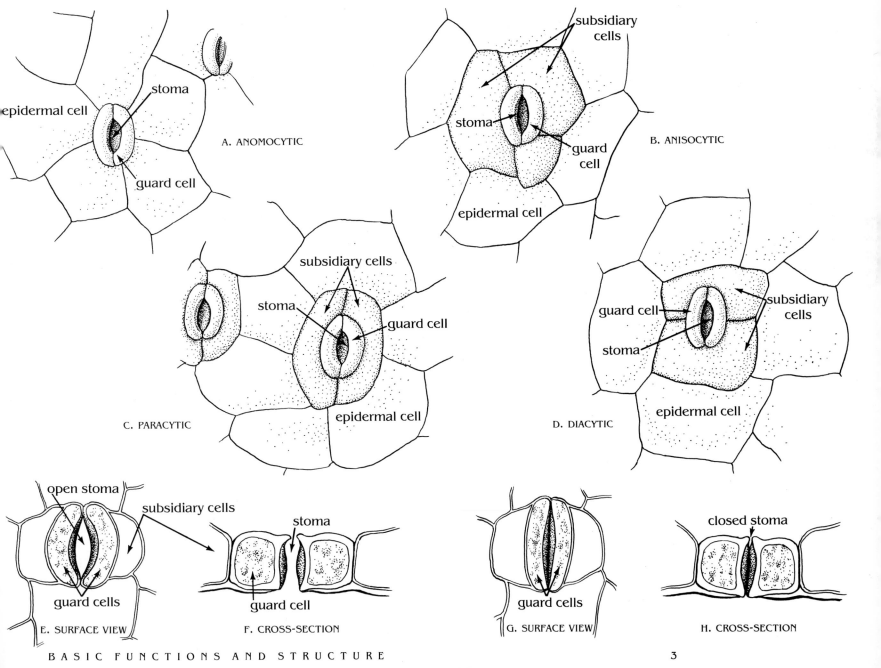

A. ANOMOCYTIC

B. ANISOCYTIC

C. PARACYTIC

D. DIACYTIC

E. SURFACE VIEW

F. CROSS-SECTION

G. SURFACE VIEW

H. CROSS-SECTION

tion in the exact layout of tissue from one plant species to another, this section shows the characteristic layers of cells that make up a typical leaf and enable it to be one of the most sophisticated chemical factories in the world.

The outside of the leaf is lined by a protective skin, or cuticle, which can often be waxy and shiny and is waterproof. Underneath the cuticle is the epidermis, or the outer layer of cells. Various structures are attached to or arise from the epidermis, especially the leaf hairs when they are present. However, most important of all are the minute pores, or stomata (a name derived from the Greek word for mouth), that are scattered all over the leaf surface, especially in the lower surface. The stomata are minute, breathing pores which can open and close, allowing gases to enter and leave the leaf. They are therefore vital to the function of the plant because it is through them that the carbon dioxide enters for photosynthesis. It is also through them that excess water vapor leaves the plant through the process of transpiration.

The stomata, like any other leaf part, are variable in their structure; however, they are usually two kidney-shaped cells that lie side by side in such a way that a small gap can open between them when the stomata open. These guard cells control the opening and closing of the stomata so that air can enter and water vapor can exit. The capacity of stomata to close is most important for plants growing in dry places where there is a water shortage. Should the stomata remain open all the time, the plant would become desiccated and die. The delicate balance of opening and closing of these tiny breathing pores is vital to the function of any plant. The stomata close down at night when the plant does not photosynthesize. Many leaves have stomata only on the lower surface, which also reduces the transpiration from the upper, sunlit surface. Stomata occur in great numbers. It is not unusual for a square inch of a typical leaf surface to have a quarter of a million of these tiny pores! For example, on a cabbage leaf there are about 652,000 stomata per square inch. This means that the whole leaf of cabbage has almost 11 million stomata. The lower surface of an apple leaf has about 161,000 stomata per square inch, whereas corn has 102,000 per square inch on the lower surface but also another 61,000 per square inch on the upper surface.

Beneath the upper epidermis there are one or more layers of rather elongate cells, called the palisade tissue. In this tightly packed tissue photosynthesis occurs. Between the palisade tissue and the lower epidermis is a layer of loosely packed, irregularly shaped cells with frequent air spaces between them to allow the gases to circulate. Naturally the intercellular air spaces lead to the stomata. The cross-section illustration shows a cut through a vein where there are two types of transport cells, the vessels that make up the xylem and the tracheids that make up the phloem. These conducting cells are surrounded by thick-walled supporting cells.

The world's green plants manufacture an estimated 200 billion tons of glucose material each year. This is not surprising when we stop to consider the surface area of the leaves of the world. A single maple tree has a trunk that covers only a square yard of ground space, yet the 100,000 leaves of the crown expose a leaf-surface area of 2,000 square yards, or half an acre.

The other vital function of leaves is transpiration, the process whereby water evaporation takes place. Most water is lost through the stomata. Through the process of transpiration the water absorbed by the roots is moved through the plant, supplying the leaves with the water they require for photosynthesis. In most plants the rate of transpiration is far greater than might be expected for the basic functioning of the plant. Plants lose a phenomenal quantity of water by transpiration. For example, a normal-sized birch tree with its 200,000 leaves will evaporate 4,560 gallons of water through its leaves in a single summer. Dr. Neil C. Turner of the Connecticut Agricultural Experiment Station in New Haven has estimated that one acre of lawn will transpire 27,000 gallons of water each week of the summer. The process of transpiration releases so much water into the atmosphere that it is a major factor in rainfall patterns. For example, Brazilian scientist Eneas Salati has calculated that 50 percent of all the rainfall of the Amazon rainforest is formed by transpiration. Thus to cut down the forest will permanently change the climate pattern of the region and accelerate drought. It is interesting that water will evaporate much more quickly from a lake surface if it is covered with aquatic plants. One of the greatest problems of some tropical lakes behind dams is infestation with the water hyacinth (*Eichhornia crassipes*), which can cover the entire lake surface. Evaporation from the leaf surface of the water hyacinth is eight times greater than that from an open water surface.

It is not surprising that plants of arid regions have many adaptations to reduce their rate of transpiration, such as reduced leaf surface, a thick cuticle, the stomata recessed below the other epidermal cells into cavities, or fewer stomata. In normally wet climates, however, plants do not have adaptations to reduce transpiration, and so in the State of Connecticut 50 billion gallons of water are transpired in a week during the summer.

What appears to the casual eye to be merely a piece of green tissue turns out to be a complex machine whose structure is closely related to its function, and whose function is of basic importance to the life of people and all animals.

Leaves are vital to life on our planet since all plants and animals are dependent on the products of photosynthesis, which provides all the energy that enables organisms to exist. The basic design of a leaf, consisting of the petiole and lamina, has naturally been modified in many ways to perform many different functions. However, as the quantity of normal, flat leaf blades around us attests, the majority of leaves are still performing the basic function of photosynthesis.

Leaf Shape and Arrangement

The great Navelwort hath round and thicke
leaves, somewhat bluntly indented about the
edges and somewhat hollow in the midst on the
upper part, having a short tender stemme fastened
to the middest of the leafe, on the lower side
underneath the stalke, whereon the flowers do grow. *

JOHN GERARD,
Herball

Leaves are many-shaped. Some are slender, smooth, and elegant; others are stubby and thick. Some have edges like ragged teeth; others are like the paw print of some large animal. They may be pointed or rounded, and to add to the profusion they are arranged in a variety of ways on the plant. They may occur in pairs, or twisted like a spiral staircase around the stems.

Taxonomists who classify plants use this variation to define and to identify plants. Consequently, they have developed an

* A description of *Cotyledon umbilicus* in the stonecrop family.

elaborate terminology to define all the different shapes, apex and base types, arrangements and grouping of leaves. Some of these shape, apex, and base types are shown in the accompanying drawings. A few of the basic leaf types and terms are defined here and full details are given in any glossary of botanical terms. The tax-onomists distinguish different plant groups by features of the flowers, fruits, and leaves. For example, many plant families, such as the birches and most oaks, have leaves which branch alternately out of the stem and are never opposite each other. Yet the maples and ash grow leaves opposite each other on the stem. Just the simple knowledge of whether a plant has opposite or alternate leaves is useful for the identification of a plant. If it has opposite leaves, there are only certain plant families to which it may belong. Other plants have their leaves arranged in a whorl or in spirals. The study of leaf arrangement on the plant is called phyllotaxy.

Types of leaf apices *(upper)* and bases *(lower),* showing some of the variety that occurs. Each type has a technical term so that it can be easily defined in a botanical description of any plant. Go out into a park or look at your houseplants and see if you can find leaves with these characteristics.

Not only is a spiral leaf arrangement beautiful and precise, but it is also useful since one leaf does not shade another. However, there is a fascinating mathematics in the spiral leaf arrangement.

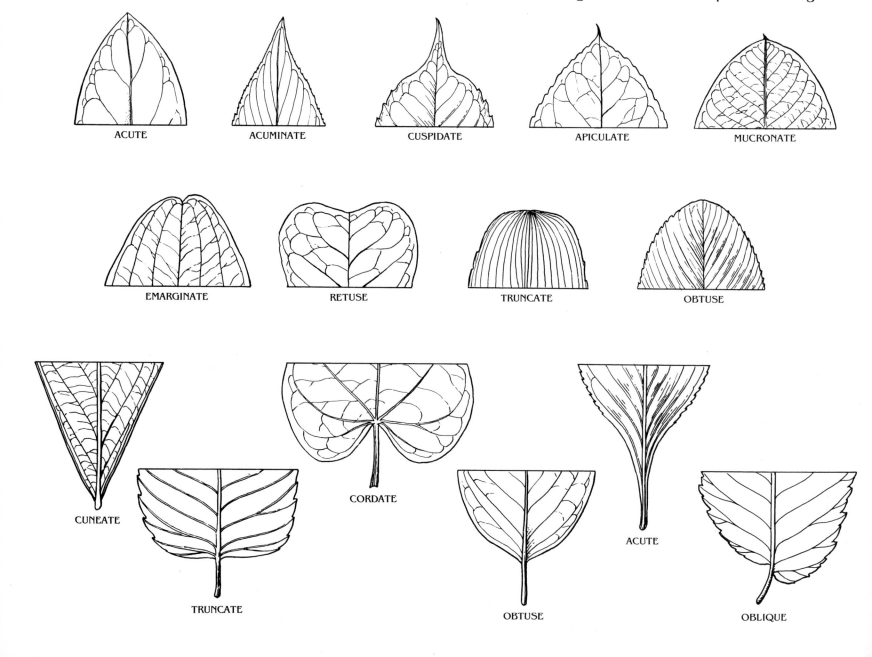

ACUTE ACUMINATE CUSPIDATE APICULATE MUCRONATE

EMARGINATE RETUSE TRUNCATE OBTUSE

CUNEATE TRUNCATE CORDATE OBTUSE ACUTE OBLIQUE

In many spirally inserted plant parts the arrangement follows a geometric series of 1, 1, 2, 3, 5, 8, 13, 21, with each succeeding number forming the sum of the preceding two. This series is called the Fibonacci numbers, after Leonardo Fibonacci, a thirteenth-century Italian mathematician, who formulated it.

Applied to plants, this number series means that if we look at certain spirally arranged leaves we find that the third leaf is directly above the first one on the stem. If it has this pattern it is called a one-third phyllotaxy. In other words, each leaf is one-third of the way around the stem from the last. Each complete circle to where two leaves coincide with each other is called a story.

In many spiral arrangements, two revolutions of the stem must be traced before one comes to leaves that are directly above the lower ones. Frequently there are five leaves inserted on this double circle. This is termed a two-fifths spiral because the pathway of the spiral has gone twice around the stem and through the bases of five leaves. Each leaf is two-fifths of the way around the stem. This pattern can be observed in the insertion on the stem of the leaves of many oaks. It can be noted that the numbers one-third and two-fifths are all in the Fibonacci series. These are simple examples, but many spirally arranged leaves and also flower parts are attached in much more complicated formulas. Each arrangement is a variation of the Fibonacci formula.

The rationale behind the spiral pattern is very practical in terms of light and space. For the plant, it is most important that one leaf not shade the leaf below it, so that each leaf receives the maximum amount of light possible. Also this geometrical pattern is a good way of packing leaves or flower parts compactly into a small space.

The normal, single leaf blade inserted directly on the stem by a leaf stalk or petiole is called a simple leaf. Many plants have compound leaves which are made up of two or more blades or leaflets. If they are featherlike with a central stem, or rachis, and have numerous lateral leaflets, they are termed pinnate. If they are handlike as in the leaves of the horse chestnut, they are palmate (see the illustration).

A. SIMPLE

B. PALMATELY COMPOUND (DIGITATE)

C. PINNATELY COMPOUND

D. BIPINNATELY COMPOUND

Leaf types. A, a simple leaf in which the leaf is formed by a single blade. B–D, types of compound leaves in which a leaf consists of a number of leaflets with a common stalk. B, palmately compound leaf where the leaflets resemble the digits of a hand. C, pinnately compound leaf with the leaflets arranged along a central stem. It is called an imparipinnate leaf because there is a terminal leaflet making the total number of leaflets an odd number. Paripinnate leaves have an even number. D, a bipinnately compound leaf where the leaf is branched and each branchlet bears a row of leaflets.

A pinnate leaf is branched once, but in some cases compound leaves are twice branched, in which case they are called bipinnate. Pinnate leaves may have a terminal leaflet so that there is an odd number of leaflets (imparipinnate), or they may have no terminal leaflets and consequently an even number of leaflets (paripinnate).

Almost all members of the numerous legume family have compound leaves. They range from the feathery leaves of many acacias and mimosas, with large numbers of small leaflets, to leaves, such as clover leaves, with just three leaflets. This type of leaflet is termed trifoliate.

The trifoliate shamrock, the national plant of Ireland, has often attracted much attention for various reasons. According to legend, Saint Patrick used the shamrock to explain the doctrine of the Trinity, as the leaf is one but is composed of three leaflets. No one is certain of the identity of the actual plant used by the saint, but it is often thought to be the wood sorrel *(Oxalis acetosella)*, although other possibilities, such as white clover *(Trifolium repens)* and black medic *(Medicago lupulina)*, are often cited as shamrock. Because of this connection between the trifoliate leaves and Saint Patrick, it has become an Irish tradition to wear the shamrock on Saint Patrick's Day.

Although the clover is usually "three-leaved" with just three leaflets, four and even five leaflets can occur. Many superstitions have been attached to the four-leaved clover, which is generally regarded as a bearer of good luck to its finder. The five-leaved clover, however, is an omen of bad luck. In Ireland, four-leaved clovers are said to grow where fairies have trod.

There are many plant families with compound leaves and others in which only simple leaves occur. The maples always have simple leaves and the legumes usually have compound leaves.

In palmate leaves, the leaflets extend from a central point rather than along a central rachis and resemble fingers arising from the palm of a hand. However, care must be taken to distinguish palmately compound leaves from digitate simple leaves which have deeply divided leaves that are not split to the base. These also have a central petiole inserted in the middle of the leaf rather than at its base as on a normal leaf; this situation is called a peltate leaf. The horse chestnut with its seven leaflets is a compound palmate leaf. The leaf of the common *Cecropia* tree of secondary areas in the New World tropics is a simple digitate leaf.

One of the most unusual leaf types is the perfoliate leaf, which as the name suggests completely surrounds the stem and is pierced by the stem, as in the small European herb the perfoliate pennycress *(Thlaspi perfoliatum)*. In perfoliate plants there is no petiole, and either one leaf has developed so that it surrounds the stem, as in the pennycress, or two opposite leaves have become fused together with no petiole to separate them from the stem, as in the member of the gentian family yellow-wort *(Blackstonia perfoliata)*. A North American example of this type of leaf is found in the thoroughwort *(Eupatorium perfolium)* in the aster family. Since this is an unusual leaf condition it is often reflected in the scientific name, as in the three examples given above.

The shapes of leaves are also used to distinguish species. Leaves vary from long, thin, narrow, lanceolate leaves of grasses and sedges to completely round or orbicular shapes with every conceivable intermediate shape, as the illustration shows. There is not usually very great variation within a single species, and its own characteristic leaf shape can be recognized readily.

Leaves of different sizes occur, varying from the sixty-foot-long fronds of some tropical palms to the pinhead-sized leaves of *Wolffia*, one of the duckweeds. One of the strangest of all leaves is that of the African desert plant *Welwitschia mirabilis* in the Gnetaceae, a strange family of cone-bearing gymnosperms. The *Welwitschia* has a short stem just above the surface which produces a pair of large opposite leaves. The leaves grow continuously and last throughout the lifetime of the plant, reaching up to seven feet in length. With time they become torn longitudinally into strips which trail along the surface of the desert. This plant is named after the German botanist Friedrich Welwitsch, who discovered the plant in 1860 in southwestern Africa.

In some plants, leaves have been lost and other organs take on the function of leaves. This is particularly common in desert plants where leaves are a disadvantage because of the water lost through them. The cacti and succulent euphorbias have no green leaves; the leaves are reduced to spines. In other plants that have lost their leaves, the stems have become leaflike and have taken up the function of photosynthesis. These leaflike stems are called cladodes. Various central Australian acacias have cladodes instead of leaves. The small European and North African genus *Ruscus*, the butcher's broom, is another good example of cladodes. The real leaves have been reduced to microscopic scales.

The diversity of leaf shapes and patterns adds to the visual richness of the world in which we live. For the plant there is a practical reason for the shape and arrangement of its leaves, and for us there is the incidental enjoyment of the ingenious designs of nature.

Variation of leaf shape showing the technical terms that are used. There are a multitude of leaf shapes and botanists have given names to each major type so that they can be easily described. The derivation of some terms is obvious, such as reniform (F) or kidney-shaped because it resembles a kidney, lanceolate (H) which is lancelike, and sagittate (K) which is like an arrowhead.

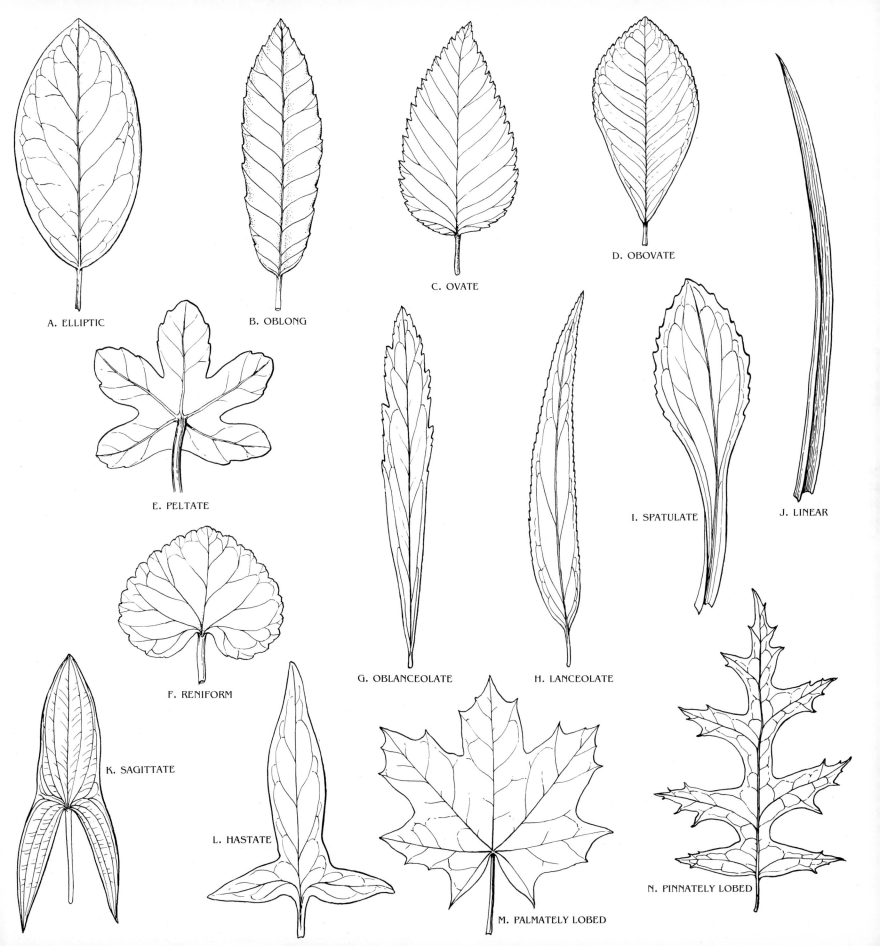

A. ELLIPTIC

B. OBLONG

C. OVATE

D. OBOVATE

E. PELTATE

F. RENIFORM

G. OBLANCEOLATE

H. LANCEOLATE

I. SPATULATE

J. LINEAR

K. SAGITTATE

L. HASTATE

M. PALMATELY LOBED

N. PINNATELY LOBED

10

ABOVE: When the petiole joins the middle of the leaf, as in this *Cecropia* from Manaus, Brazil, it is termed peltate.

OPPOSITE PAGE, LEFT: The simple leaves of a member of the coffee family *(Mussaenda erythrophylla)* from Zaire are arranged opposite each other.

OPPOSITE PAGE, RIGHT: The simple leaves of an *Apama* from Sri Lanka are arranged alternately on the stem.

ABOVE: The spiral leaves of a minute sedge from Chiang Mai, Thailand. The total diameter is only one inch.

OPPOSITE PAGE, LEFT: The compound leaf or frond of a tree fern.

LEAF SHAPE AND ARRANGEMENT

TOP RIGHT: The stem of this *Costus* in the ginger family is spiral.

BOTTOM RIGHT: The leaves of *Dendrobium leonis* from New Guinea are distichous, arranged in two planes only.

LEAF SHAPE AND ARRANGEMENT

ABOVE: A leaf of the tree alfalfa *(Medicago arborea)* is compound, consisting of three leaflets. Compound leaves with three leaflets are termed trifoliolate.

BELOW: The leaves of a fascinating aquatic member of the mimosa family, *Neptunia oleracea,* are compound and pinnate.

LEAF SHAPE AND ARRANGEMENT

OPPOSITE PAGE, TOP RIGHT: The flamboyant tree, *Delonix regia,* has a pinnate leaf.

OPPOSITE PAGE, BOTTOM RIGHT: This *Cecropia* leaf is simple because it is not completely divided into leaflets. Leaves of this sort are digitate, or fingerlike.

BELOW: A spirally arranged leaf of *Aeonium haworthii* in the stonecrop family is a good demonstration of phyllotaxy, or leaf arrangement.

ABOVE AND OPPOSITE PAGE, RIGHT: The traveler's palm is not really a palm and has the leaves arranged in a distinctive pattern in a single plane.

LEAF SHAPE AND ARRANGEMENT

LEFT: In *Begonia duartei* the leaf itself is spiral.

ABOVE: The bur reed *Sparganium* has narrow, alternate leaves.

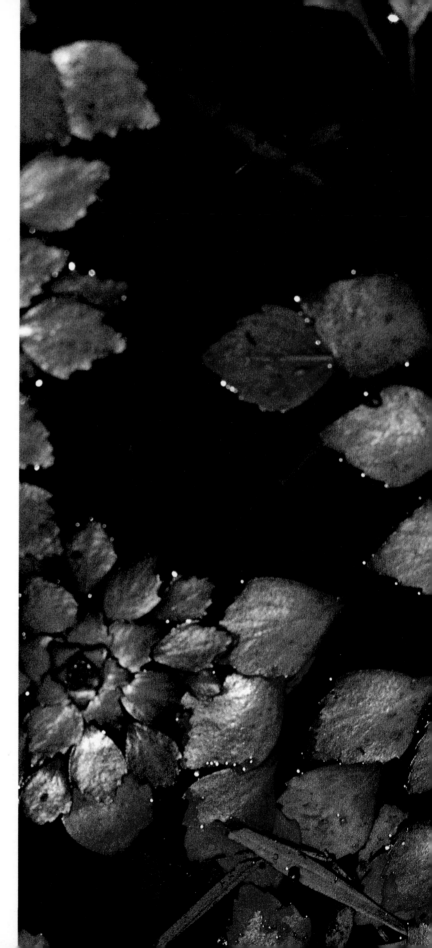

RIGHT: The spiral leaves of the aquatic *Ludwigia natans* from Amazonian Brazil.

The leaf of a fan palm, *Licuala grandis,* from New Britain Islands.
The palm leaves are folded like a fan in bud, which is termed
plicate.

LEAF SHAPE AND ARRANGEMENT

CHAPTER 3

Veins: The Plumbing of a Leaf

One of the best ways to examine leaf venation is to find a partially decomposed leaf on a forest floor with much of the leaf tissue rotted away, leaving only its skeleton of nerves or veins. The veins are made of strong material with thick cells to support them and to enable them to function properly. When a leaf falls to the forest floor it often loses the soft cells and only the nerves remain, leaving a delicate, lacelike structure. Some insects also make leaf skeletons by eating away the soft tissue and leaving the veins. In leaf fossils it is often only the veins that remain apparent. This has made the detailed study of venation most important so that paleobotanists, the plant fossil specialists, can identify to what species their fossil belongs. By looking closely at a leaf one can see that it is covered with a series of veins or nerves. These are the internal transport mechanism of the plant through which the different substances move to and from the leaves and the stem. There is much variation in the pattern of these veins and this tells us a great deal about the different plants.

The most basic division of leaf types is into parallel veined and net veined. These also correspond approximately with the two major divisions of seed plants, the monocotyledons, with one seedling leaf and parallel-veined leaves, and the dicotyledons, with net-veined leaves and two seedling leaves. The grasses with their narrow, lancelike leaves have a series of parallel veins running throughout their length parallel to the margins. The majority of trees, however, have a single central vein or midrib and a series of veins that run toward the margin with a fine network of small veins in between the principal branches.

A detailed system of classification of leaf venation has been worked out, with a series of terms to describe each possible variation of vein pattern. For example, a simple parallel vein pattern is called parallelodromous. A net-veined leaf where the secondary branch veins run right to the margins is called craspedodromous, but if the veins arch over to join each other before the margins it is brochidodromous. If the secondary veins end before the margins without uniting they are then eucamptodromous. Pick up the leaves of a few plants around you and look at the amazing variety of leaf venation that you will find. A few families of dicotyledons have more than one principal vein and these are more or less parallel to one another. For example, this acrodromous type of venation is characteristic of one of the largest tropical plant families, the Melastomataceae, of which the single genus *Rhexia*, the meadow beauty, reaches the northeastern United States.

Between the secondary veins the pattern of the tertiary veins and their branches also form a countless variety of patterns, varying from distinctly parallel arrangements to most complicated reticulate patterns. In some cases the reticulations are ordered into quite definite, constantly repeated patterns, whereas in others they are much more randomly arranged.

One of the strangest of all leaves must be that of the Madagascan lattice-leaf *(Aponogeton fenestrale)*. This large-leaved water plant is like a series of green lace frills decorating the ponds because it grows naturally as a leaf skeleton. The leaves consist of the central midrib, an outer marginal nerve, and an intricate network of veins. However, the tissue between the veins is missing in this remarkable curiosity of nature. It is well named *fenestrale*, after the Latin for window *(fenestra)*, because the leaf is a series of open windows with only the frame in position. The lattice-leaf is one of the best known natural demonstrations of leaf venation.

Leaf veins are the plant's lifeline, but incidentally serve to aid the taxonomist who seeks to classify plants. Many species can be identified by their own specific "fingerprint," the leaf vein pattern.

RIGHT: The plant family Melastomataceae is one of the easiest tropical groups to recognize because of its distinct venation, with several parallel principal nerves, technically termed acrodromous. This photograph was taken near Manaus, Brazil.

The leaf of this *Sauvagesia glandulosa* has a very strong marginal nerve. This member of the ochna family is from Brazil.

ABOVE: The venation pattern of the leaf of the cashew nut tree (*Anacardium occidentale*).

BOTTOM RIGHT: A fall leaf of the wild black cherry (*Prunus* species) shows the commonest vein pattern, single central nerve and numerous side branches.

VEINS: THE PLUMBING OF A LEAF

TOP: A technique for the study of leaf venation is to clear the leaves chemically, often with sodium hydroxide. The leaf becomes clear and is then stained with a dye that emphasizes the venation. A relative of the Brazil nut, *Couratari tenuicarpa* from Brazil, with a typical network of venation.

BELOW: Leaf venation often becomes apparent through the work of insects that eat out the soft tissue and leave behind the skeleton of the leaf.

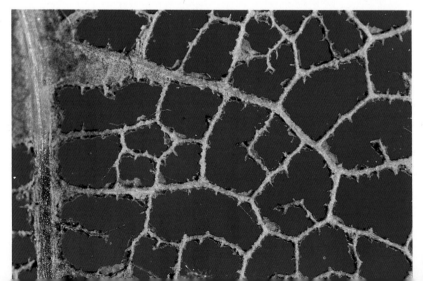

ABOVE: A member of the plant family Melastomataceae. This photograph was taken near Manaus, Brazil.

LEFT: The lower surface of the leaf of *Callicarpa tomentosa* in the verbena family from Sri Lanka, where it is used as a disinfectant.

VEINS: THE PLUMBING OF A LEAF

ABOVE: The complex venation of the compound leaf of a member of the carrot family, *Chaerophyllum villarsii,* from Germany.

BELOW: The venation of *Sassafras variifolium* photographed in New Jersey.

BELOW: Variegated leaves often emphasize the venation pattern, as in this *Codiaeum variegatum undulatum* in the spurge family from Java.

VEINS: THE PLUMBING OF A LEAF

RIGHT: The parallel venation of the bromeliad *Vriesea platynema* from Amazonia.

BELOW: The leaf of *Alangium* from China showing several veins arising from the leaf base in a palmate pattern.

RIGHT: The prickly leaf of *Maytenus ilicifolia* of the bittersweet family from Brazil.

BOTTOM RIGHT: The parallel venation on part of a leaf of the palm *Hyospathe* from Manaus, Brazil.

BELOW: A skeletonized leaf from the forest floor of Amazonia. The soft tissue has all rotted away, leaving only the intricate system of veins which once transported nutrients around the leaf.

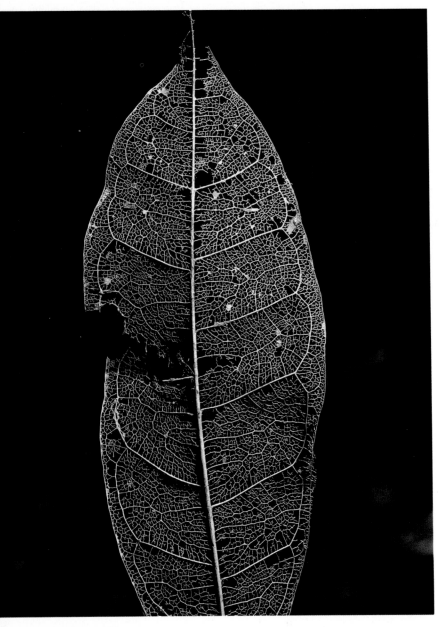

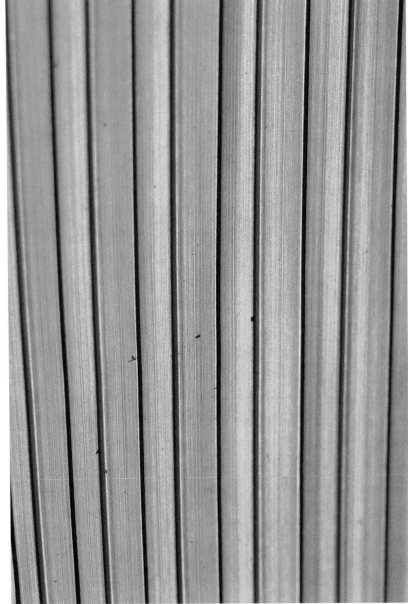

VEINS: THE PLUMBING OF A LEAF

RIGHT: Detail of the veins of the apical portion of an Amazonian leaf.

BELOW: The large group of plants called monocotyledons mostly have parallel venation rather than a network. This is *Setaria,* a grass from Ghana with parallelodromous venation.

ABOVE: The leaf of *Alchemilla filicaulis* from Canada with a palmate pattern.

CHAPTER 4

Leaf Margins

There thistles stretch their prickly arms afar,
And to the ragged infant threaten war;
There poppies, nodding, much the hope of toil;
There the blue bugloss paints the sterile soil;
Hardy and high, above the slender sheaf,
The slimy mallow waves her silky leaf.

GEORGE CRABBE,
"The Village"

Leaves may have any one of a variety of shapes, but nature's ingenuity is also displayed in the way in which leaves with the same shape may have different margins or edges. Nature's variations are not haphazard, and it is often possible to discover the reason for or purpose behind the kind of edge on a leaf.

Prickly margins, as shown in the illustration, are familiar. The holly has sharp prickles at irregular intervals around the edge of the leaves.* Thistles, too, have similar prickles on their leaf margins. A well-browsed pasture usually has a stand of pristine thistles, and this is connected with the fact that the sharp woody spines are a deterrent to any browsing animal. The prickly margin

* Prickles are actually outgrowths of the leaf's vein endings.

serves as a defense against animals which would eat the plant. The prickles, however, do not always protect the plant against insect predators.

The leaf margins of various sedges are most unpleasant to the uninitiated hiker or hunter because they can be razor-sharp. The margin consists of minute, hardened, sawlike teeth which will cut anything that brushes against them. Examples of this include *Cladium mariscus*, a sedge of marshlands that is widely distributed in the temperate region. In the tropics the sedges called razor-grass (*Scleria* species) are the best example. The term *razor* is apt, but the plant is really a sedge, not a grass, and so the second half of the common name is a misnomer. However, sedges and grasses have look-alike thin, narrow, parallel-veined leaves. They can be distinguished because most sedges have a triangular solid stem, whereas grasses have a round stem which is hollow between the nodes, or joints, on the stem.

Razor "grass" trails over low vegetation in the forests of Amazonia, especially in disturbed secondary areas. It has the habit of clinging to one's clothing and, since it is so sharp, cuts both clothes and skin. It is one of the more noxious plants of the Amazon forest. The local name is tiririca vine, which is derived from the Tupi word *tirica* (to break open or split), an appropriate name because it describes just what the plant does.

The margin of the leaves, especially of tropical trees, is extended into a finely pointed tip. On a rainy day when the water is running off the apex, the function of these pointed tips can be seen. This drip tip, as it is called, helps the water to drain off the leaf surface after the heavy tropical rains. Long after rainfall has ceased, the forest appears to be receiving a shower as the leaves continue to drip from their tips until all the water has run off. If the leaves did not have these drip tips, water could accumulate and its weight could cause damage both to the individual leaves and to the branches, which could break under the weight of excess water. This drip-tip modification is an important adaptation to the tropical rainforest environment.

The commonest type of leaf margin is one which has no distinctive features and is even all the way around. This is called an entire margin. If the margin is wavy but not toothed, it is then undulate. When it is toothed, it is either serrate (sawlike) or dentate (toothlike). Serrate margins have rather even and sawlike pointed teeth around them, and dentate margins have wider-spaced teeth that are pointed outward. If the teeth are blunt or rounded, then the margin is said to be crenate. Finally, if the leaf is really divided from the margin it is pinnatilobed. These technical terms and various others for intermediate forms appear frequently in botanical description of plants, and are illustrated in the figure.

Leaf margins are highly variable and furnish useful taxonomic characters for species. A leaf with a straight margin with no divisions is termed entire (A), and one that has teeth like a saw is serrate (D). Look at the leaves around you and examine the margins to find the variation.

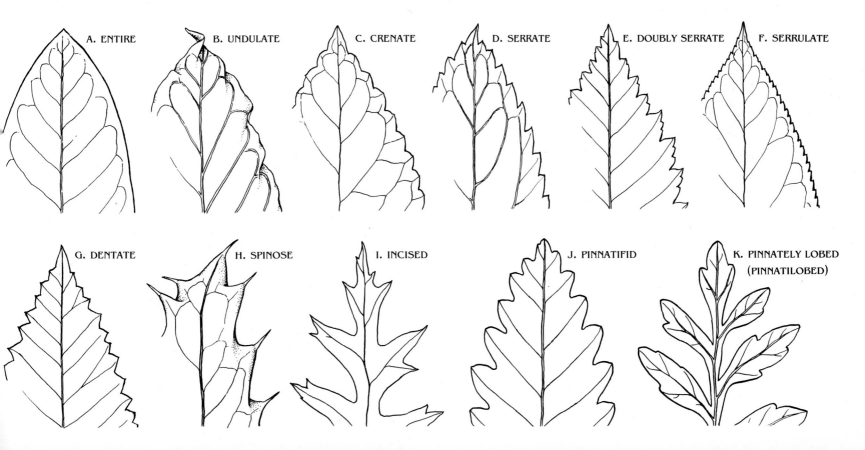

A. ENTIRE   B. UNDULATE   C. CRENATE   D. SERRATE   E. DOUBLY SERRATE   F. SERRULATE

G. DENTATE   H. SPINOSE   I. INCISED   J. PINNATIFID   K. PINNATELY LOBED (PINNATILOBED)

BELOW: Wavy or undulate leaf margin in *Elettaria cardamomum*, the cardamom spice, photographed in Sri Lanka.

TOP RIGHT: The simple leaf margin of the rubber plant *(Ficus elastica)*, a common houseplant native of India.

BOTTOM RIGHT: A cleared leaf of *Desfontainea spinosa*, named for the protective spines of the leaf margins. *Desfontainea*, a rare genus of the Andes, belongs to its own plant family, the Desfontaineaceae.

LEFT: A cleared leaf of *Potentilla atrorubens* with a serrate margin.

BELOW: The Latin name of *Callicoma serratifolia* from Australia refers to the sawlike teeth around the leaf margin, seen here in a cleared and stained leaf.

BELOW: The undulate and variegated leaf margin of the bromeliad *Cryptanthus* from Amazonian Brazil.

The attractive margin of *Acalypha godseffiana* from Sumatra.

LEFT: An entire simple leaf margin of a rainforest leaf from near Manaus, Brazil. This is also a good example of the drip tip of a leaf apex characteristic of many rainforest trees.

ABOVE: When a leaf margin is toothed like a saw it is termed serrate, as in this *Pilea involucrata* in the nettle family, from Peru.

LEFT: The leaves of the much cultivated plant *Olmediella* are very similar to those of the familiar holly. This native of Central America is now known only in cultivation.

RIGHT: The basal part of this Amazon rainforest leaf is spinous.

BELOW: The toothed or dentate margin of this *Bryophyllum pinnatum* from India is highlighted by the natural red color.

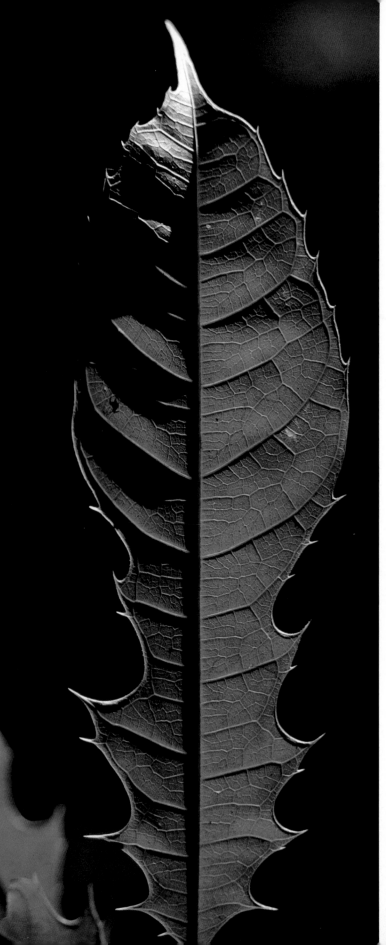

36

RIGHT: The leaf margins of the rare *Luxemburgia gardneri* from Brazil have long, protruding hairs.

BELOW: Leaf margins often become spinous as in this *Polyscias guilfoylei* from Polynesia.

Cotyledons: The Seed Leaves of Plants

The store of nutriment laid up within the seeds of many plants seems at first sight to have no sort of relation to other plants. But from such seeds (as peas and beans), when sown in the midst of long grass, I suspect that the chief use of the nutriment in the seed is to favour the growth of the young seedling, whilst struggling with other plants growing vigorously all around.

CHARLES DARWIN,
On the Origin of Species

The two major divisions of the seed plants, or angiosperms, are called monocotyledons and dicotyledons (usually termed monocots and dicots for short). This name refers to a leaf characteristic because a cotyledon is the seed leaf of a plant. They are the leaves of the embryo which have become adapted to a variety of functions. As the names would imply, the monocots usually have a single-seed leaf, whereas the dicots have two. The monocots are plants like grasses, lilies, orchids, and irises. Many of them also have narrow, lancelike leaves with parallel venation. The dicots usually have two cotyledons and net-veined leaves with a single principal nerve. There are a few exceptional plants that have a different number of cotyledons. For example, one of the most primitive of all the dicots, *Degeneria vitiensis* from Fiji, has three or four cotyledons arranged in a whorl around the stem.

The seed leaves usually look quite different from the later leaves of a plant because their functions are different. Often the seed leaves store food. Perhaps you have seen a lima bean germinate. The two large, fleshy cotyledons push above the soil and the shoot grows from between them. The cotyledons of the bean provide nourishment to the young, developing plant. As the plant becomes established and its real leaves begin to gather energy through photosynthesis, the cotyledons wither and fall off. Their task is performed; they have provided food to the seedling through the critical period of its initial growth, before it was equipped to make its food by photosynthesis.

The bean is an example of cotyledons that are pushed up above the ground on the seedling stem. This is called epigeal germination. This term is derived from the Greek words *epi,* meaning over, and *ge,* meaning earth. Many familiar words involving earth sciences begin with *ge,* such as *geography, geology,* and *geode.* In many other plants, the cotyledons remain inside the seed in the soil and just the shoot is pushed up through the soil. This is termed hypogeal, *hypo* being the Greek word for under. Various plants use the same word in their species names where underground features are important. For example, the peanut is called *Arachis hypogaea* because the peanuts develop *under* the ground.

Whether the cotyledons remain underground or push upward above the soil, they can function as a food storage for the seedling. In some plants, however, the cotyledons are small and the seedling has a separate tissue for the food storage, called endosperm. This starchy tissue is developed as the seed is formed after fertilization of the flower. Some groups of plants supply food to their seedling through an endosperm and others through storage in the seed leaves. These are two different ways that germinating seedlings provide and store the energy for growth until they are capable of manufacturing food.

In the germination of a seed, cotyledons have one of two possible functions. Either they serve as foliage leaves to begin photosynthesis for the new plant, or they are fleshy food-storage organs which often remain underground. This difference in function was hinted at by the famous botanist A. P. de Candolle in 1825 when he observed that swollen cotyledons do not possess stomata and so their function is obviously not primarily photosynthesis but food storage.

The gymnosperms, or cone-bearing plants, such as the firs and pines, have many cotyledons. The lower plants which produce spores instead of seeds do not have any cotyledons, and are termed acotyledonous. The cotyledons of the conifers have a third function other than storage and photosynthesis, termed haustorial. That is, they function like the food-absorbing organs of parasites. They extend into the endosperm storage tissue and function like a root, transferring the nutrients of the endosperm to the rest of the seedling. This kind of seed-leaf function is common in Cycads and in the Chinese Maidenhair tree *(Ginkgo).* This type of cotyledon is usually opaque in color since green chlorophyll is not necessary for it to function.

The way in which cotyledons, especially foliar ones, are folded in the seed is extremely varied. For example, those of *Cordia,* a common tropical genus of trees, are plicate, or folded like a fan. In *Terminalia* they are rolled up, and in *Cariniana,* in the Brazil nut family, they are coiled inwardly over themselves in a most complex pattern.

The cotyledons of many plants are relatively simple individual structures and seldom resemble the later leaves of the plant. However, there is considerable variation in the morphology of cotyledons apart from the basic differences connected with their function (storage, foliar, or haustorial). Some cotyledons are narrow and lanceolate; others are broad and bear a greater resemblance to a leaf blade. In some plants, such as many members of the mustard family (Brassicaceae), the two cotyledons are unequal. They are generally entire, but in some plants, such as the *Pelargonium,* they are lobed. They are usually without a leaf stalk, but cotyledons with a petiole do occur in some species.

When you next see a seedling germinate, such as one of the many maple seeds that settle down on a lawn or park, examine their germination and look for the two epigeal, or above-ground, cotyledons that appear and are quickly followed by the first pair of leaves.

Since cotyledons are often the food-storage organs of the leaves, they provide useful products for people. Many seeds that are eaten or used for some other purpose are useful because of the substances stored in their cotyledons. For example, the cotyledons of *Acioa edulis,* illustrated in this chapter, are full of oils. The fruits of this Amazonian plant are collected by natives and may be cracked open and eaten like nuts or the cotyledons removed and pressed to extract an oil which is used in cooking or to make soap. The Mexicans use the cotyledons of a related species, *Licania arborea,* or the cacahuananche tree. The cotyledons of this tree are rich in a flammable oil which is often strung on sticks for illuminating purposes. The light passes along the chain from one fruit to the next. The oil is also extracted commercially for use in candles, soap, and axle grease.

Beans and peas are nutritious vegetables because of the rich supply of protein and other nutrients that are stored in their cotyledons. However, in cereals such as wheat and corn the cotyledons are small and the rich supply of carbohydrate is stored in the form of endosperm, the other way in which seeds store their nutrient supplies.

Cotyledons are of great importance to people because of the number of seed plants in which they are used. The legume family alone is second only to grasses in importance as a source of food, most of which comes from the cotyledons. A few examples include beans, peas, lentils, soybeans, and peanuts.

The Seedling and Embryo of Acioa edulis, *a Tropical Tree from Amazonia*

The cotyledons are epigeal, that is, they emerge above the soil. They are thick and fleshy, indicating that their primary purpose is the storage of food. The cotyledons of *A. edulis* contain so much oil that it is an important source of cooking oil for some Amazonian natives.

ABOVE: This plant has a pair of large foliaceous, or leaflike, cotyledons (seed leaves) whose obvious purpose is to begin photosynthesis quickly for the seedling while the shoot and new leaves develop.

THE SEED LEAVES OF PLANTS

The seedling of A. edulis showing the cotyledons below the first leaves. Once the leaves are established and photosynthesizing their own energy, the cotyledons will fall.

The embryo of A. edulis opened up to show how the young shoot and the first leaves are protected and folded up between the two large cotyledons.

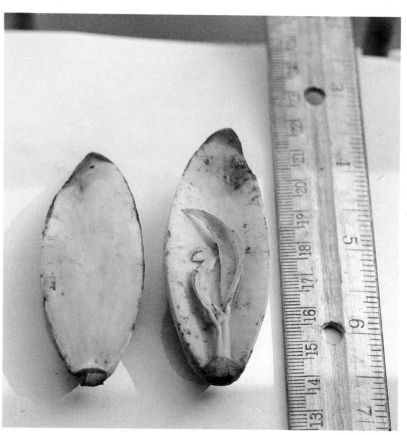

CHAPTER 6

Young Leaves: How and Why They Look Different

Oh to be in England
Now that April's there
And whoever wakes in England
Sees, some morning, unaware,
That the lowest boughs and the brushwood sheaf
Round the elm-tree bole are in tiny leaf.

ROBERT BROWNING,
"Home Thoughts from Abroad"

The bud on the bough again,
The leaf on the tree.

CHARLES JEFFREY,
"The Meeting of Spring and Summer"

Newborn leaves emerge rapidly from the buds of their plant, but they are usually rather different from the mature leaves. Immature leaves are soft and limp and often hang down as if they were wilted. It takes some time for them to become stiff and ready to support themselves in an upright position. Frequently the color of new leaves is different from that of their adult phase. They are often red, yellow, or bluish because they still lack chlorophyll. Once they unfurl and begin to produce chlorophyll, the red pigments are obscured by the abundant chlorophyll being produced and they turn green. The red coloring is particularly apparent in the young leaves of the tropical rainforest, where almost all the trees produce colored new leaves. However, it is also common to see shades of yellow, red, and blue in the leaves of the trees of the temperate forest.

Scientists have hypothesized that perhaps the different color of young leaves is advantageous to them because they do not appear attractive to insects and are thus afforded some protection against insect predators at the time when they are vulnerable because of their immaturity.

In bud, leaves are folded in many different ways and consequently they unfurl differently. For example, the leaves of most palms are folded exactly like the pleats of a fan. This type of pattern is termed plicate, and occurs mainly in the palms and the "Panama hat" family (Cyclanthaceae). The leaves of many members of the maranta family (Marantaceae) are rolled up in a cylinder and pushed up in a tube which later unfolds once it is well above ground. One of the most attractive juvenile leaf bud arrangements is that of the familiar fiddlehead ferns, so-called because of the resemblance of this tightly coiled frond to the scroll at the head of a fiddle, or violin. The fiddleheads are leaf buds of ferns which emerge from the soil and uncoil to form the mature fronds. Many different ferns produce fiddleheads, whether they are tiny ground ferns of New England or gigantic tree ferns of the tropical forests of Australia or Fiji.

The fiddleheads of at least one species, the ostrich fern *(Matteuccia struthiopteris)* of New England, are eaten as an asparagus-like delicacy. The ostrich-fern fiddleheads appear in early spring and are usually snipped off when they are about three inches tall. They are steamed, boiled, or sautéed and are a favorite spring vegetable of Maine and New Brunswick. The fiddleheads are technically named crosiers because of the resemblance to a bishop's staff.

RIGHT: The young, limp leaf of a common Amazon tree, *Scleronema micranthum,* known in Brazil as the cardeiro.

ABOVE: Young leaves of *Tristania conferta* from Java.

LEFT: The young leaf of a rainforest plant in Java with typical red coloration.

BELOW: Young leaves and tendrils of an Amazonian passion flower vine near Manaus, Brazil.

BELOW: Raindrops enhance the beauty of this Amazonian rainforest leaf from Manaus, Brazil.

BELOW: The new leaves of *Pometia pinnata* from Fiji.

ABOVE: Young leaves of *Pometia pinnata* from Fiji.

YOUNG LEAVES

TOP RIGHT: The fiddlehead of the fern *Cyathea crinata* has a shaggy appearance because of the number of hairlike scales.

BOTTOM RIGHT: The young leaves of tree cinnamon *(Cinnamomum)* from Sri Lanka, a much-used spice.

BELOW: The fiddlehead, or crozier, of the fern of the *Blechnum* species, which is the rolled-up leaf bud.

BELOW: These young leaves of *Dipterocarpus zeylanicus* from Sri Lanka are both red and soft when they first emerge.

ABOVE: The young opening leaf of a rainforest plant from Sabah.

LEFT: This fern of the *Blechnum* species from Sri Lanka has red young fronds that unroll like fiddleheads.

RIGHT: The compound leaves of the Leguminosae have complicated buds with many compactly stored leaflets.

BELOW: This beautiful purple color is from the young leaf of *Gynura aurantiaca*, or the velvet plant, a member of the aster family.

ABOVE: A leaf of *Dipteris* fern from Mount Kinabalu in Sabah.

OPPOSITE PAGE, TOP LEFT: This unusual leaf of *Dipteris* fern is from Mount Kinabalu in Sabah.

OPPOSITE PAGE, BOTTOM LEFT: The sunlight in a forest catches the colored undersurface of this young palm leaf near Manaus, Brazil.

OPPOSITE PAGE, RIGHT: The leaves of most members of the Maranta family (Marantaceae) emerge as a tube which unrolls once it is above soil level, as in this *Calathea lindeniana* from Brazil.

YOUNG LEAVES

CHAPTER 7

Variegated Leaves

It farre exceedeth my skill to describe the beauty and excellence of this rare plant called Floramor; and I think that the pensil of the most curious painter will be at a stay, when he shall come to set it downe in lively colours. . . . Whereupon doth grow many leaves, wherein doth consist the beauty: for in a few words, everie leafe resembleth in colour the most faire and beautifull feather of a Parat especially those feathers that are mixed with most sundry colours, as a stripe of red, and a line of yellow, a dash of white, and a rib of green colour which I cannot with words set forth, such are the sundry mixtures of colours that Nature hath bestowed in her greatest jolitie, upon this floure.

JOHN GERARD,
Herball

The majority of plants have plain green leaves in order to maximize their capacity for photosynthesis. However, there are a considerable number of different plant species that have a mixture of colors on their leaves. Such plants are called variegated. These variegated leaves are particularly common in plants of the tropical forest, but they have become well known to us because they are often cultivated. The variety of patterns on the foliage of variegated plants is fascinating and it adds a welcome bit of color for those who have become bored with plain green foliage. The leaves may have dots of white, vivid patches of red, or different colors on the upper and lower surfaces. In some cases there may be a mixture of white, red, and pink; others are almost all white with a little of the green chlorophyll which they need for photosynthesis. Variegated leaves add color to the wonderful world of leaves. Perhaps you are familiar with variegated coleus, aspidistra, caladium, or begonias, just to mention a few of the commonly grown plants that have this type of leaf pattern.

Why, when a leaf is busy gathering sunlight for photosynthesis, would it have developed areas lacking chlorophyll that are incapable of contributing to the process? The answers to that question are many, because variegated leaves have evolved for a variety of good reasons.

If you have cultivated variegated houseplants you may have had problems with the maintenance of vivid color differences because some variegated plants lose their variegations when placed in bright light. In contrast, and to complicate their cultivation, other variegated plants become much more brightly variegated when placed in the sun and become green when in the shade. However, as long as you know which ones act which way you should have no trouble, because they are consistent within an individual variety. Some plants need to receive direct light each day and others grow better in continuous shade. This is even true of forest trees; some grow rapidly toward the light whenever there is a light gap caused by a fallen tree, yet other species grow steadily upward in the shade of the upper story of the forest. Plants that require strong light will tend to lose their variegation when placed in the shade. The leaves are compensating for the lack of light and increasing the area that is active in photosynthesis. In contrast, plants that are shade-loving will compensate through the reverse process and will tend to increase the degree of variation.

In this phenomenon we can see two of the reasons for variegations. Shade-loving plants that receive too much light had to become variegated to reduce the area of functional leaf. This type of variegation is most frequently green and white, the white areas being the ones that have no chlorophyll. This happens when forest-floor species occur in lighter areas, such as on the edge of clearings. Light-demanding variegated species must have their color pattern for other reasons. One of these may be to absorb light from different parts of the light spectrum and thus maximize their efficiency. Green chlorophyll will only gather part of the available light. The plants that are variegated to gather a wider range of light tend to have more vivid colors, usually the reds and pinks.

Another rather common phenomenon of deep-shade plants in rainforests is a deep, iridescent-blue leaf color. This is particularly noticeable in some species of the fern ally *Selaginella*, but occurs in many other plants, such as the sedge genus *Mapania*. Studies of the anatomy of the leaves of iridescent plants by scientist David W. Lee showed that where green iridescence occurs it is due to the refraction of diffuse light onto specially oriented chloroplasts by lens-shaped cells. Where the iridescence is blue it is caused by the operation of thin-film interference filters in the leaf epidermis. To have such a mechanism is a great advantage to plants of the deeply shaded forest floor because it gives them the ability to absorb red wavelengths of light rather than the less important blue wavelengths. This phenomenon seems to have developed mostly in ferns.

There are other, most interesting reasons for variegated plants to occur. Numerous plants have brightly colored leaves to attract pollinators. Just as the leaves or bracts near the flower of the poinsettia, described in Chapter 16, seem to attract pollinators, other plants have variegated leaves. Two of the photographs on page 60 show a gesneriad, or member of the African violet family, with bright-red leaf apices. The tubular flowers are hidden under the leaf and the hummingbird pollinators are attracted to probe under the leaves by their bright-red patches. When the sun from a sun fleck in the forest strikes these leaves they stand out conspicuously and would certainly be attractive to hummingbirds, which invariably come to red objects. On one occasion we marked a forest trail in the Amazon with red tape. We were amazed to see how frequently hummingbirds came to investigate these red objects scattered throughout the forest.

Caladiums are often cultivated for their variegated leaves. These plants have small and inconspicuous flowers; their variegated leaves are what attract the pollinating insects. Some plants become variegated only near flowering time. This color change, timed to coincide with the period when the plant needs to attract pollinators, is the best evidence that variegation can be for the purpose of pollinator attraction. One of the best examples of this is another frequently cultivated bromeliad, *Neoregelia* (see photograph, page 63). When the plant approaches flowering time, the center leaves that surround the inflorescence turn a bright scarlet color which also attracts hummingbirds. Brightly colored leaves are a common phenomenon in the bromeliads.

Another reason for variegation is to warn predatory insects that the leaves taste bad. Many of the most brightly colored organisms are bad-tasting. Once a bird or an insect has taken a bite from a certain leaf it will remember that leaf better if it is distinctive. Variegated patterns can serve to advertise the fact that these leaves are unpleasant, and consequently they get little predation. There are also many animals that use the same mechanism, such as the coral snake, or brightly colored butterflies like the monarch. Other animals have gradually evolved similar patterns because they too are avoided by predators that have experienced the bad-tasting species. Natural selection has favored their survival; the more like the noxious animal, the more chance of survival. There is a false coral snake which closely resembles the true coral, and many foul-tasting butterflies have harmless look-alikes. This phenomenon is called mimicry. When a nontoxic organism resembles a toxic one it is termed Batesian mimicry, after the great naturalist Henry W. Bates who spent many years in the Amazon forest and first described the occurrence of mimicry in butterflies. Thus the variegation of some leaves is a warning to herbivorous animals.

Variegation is not a simple phenomenon. We have now seen at least four different reasons for it to occur, so it is hardly surprising that there are many variegated plants in the world with a great variety of different patterns and colors of variegation.

The mechanisms of how a plant can have a variegated leaf are also interesting and diverse. Leaves actually contain a variety of pigments in addition to the green chlorophyll. In the discussion of fall coloring, in Chapter 17, we will see what happens when the chlorophyll ceases to be made in a leaf. Carotene is a yellow-orange pigment and anthocyanin a red to blue pigment. The visibility of anthocyanin rather than chlorophyll is the commonest mechanism for a variegated leaf. Since these different pigments are closely related chemically it is comparatively easy for a plant to produce variegated leaves through rather minor chemical changes. Variegated leaves can also be caused by viral infection or because of mineral deficiencies, and some patterns are caused by the alteration of the cell structure of the leaf. For example, the presence of airspaces under the leaf surface and a thin epidermis will cause spots or patches that look a different color.

Some variegated plants are made up of two separate tissues. Such a plant is termed a chimaera, after the creature of Greek mythology that was supposed to have the head of a lion, the middle section of a goat, and the rear part of a dragon. In other words, the leaf has a mixture of tissues. Plant breeders have been able to mix green and white tissues to produce artificially variegated plants. One chimaera which is frequently cultivated is variegated maple. Owners of the cultivar of the box-maple *Acer negundo* cultivar *variegatum* have frequently been disappointed by the fact that this variegated form reverts to plain leaves. In this case the inner core of the leaves is of the ordinary *A. negundo* type and only the outer layer is of the other tissue type which produces the variegated leaves. Pruning will often cause the inner layer to break through and the leaves will revert to a green color. If you have a variegated maple of this type, avoid pruning and it will lessen the risk of reversion to the "plain Jane" type. The variegated box maple is a most attractive tree with white to silver leaf margins.

Variegated plants have been despised by some growers as freaks, but to others they have great appeal because they add a dash of color to a dull landscape or to a drab collection of green houseplants. Ordinary-looking and unexciting leaves can be turned into sources of great interest and attraction if they have an attractive, variegated pattern. There are now many variegated cultivars available so that it is easy to find examples both for indoors and for the garden.

VARIEGATED LEAVES

OPPOSITE PAGE, LEFT, AND ABOVE: The multicolored, variegated pattern of *Maranta leuconeura* makes it an attractive houseplant. The Latin name means red-nerved.

TOP RIGHT: The variegation of this *Aphelandra squarrosa* from Brazil is caused by the absence of green chlorophyll along the venation.

BELOW: *Coleus* is a much-cultivated genus. This *Coleus rehneltianus,* known as the red trailing queen, is from Sri Lanka.

BELOW: A similar pattern of white venation on the nerve plant, *Fittonia verschaffeltii* var. *argyroneura,* from Ecuador. This houseplant is best cultivated in a terrarium.

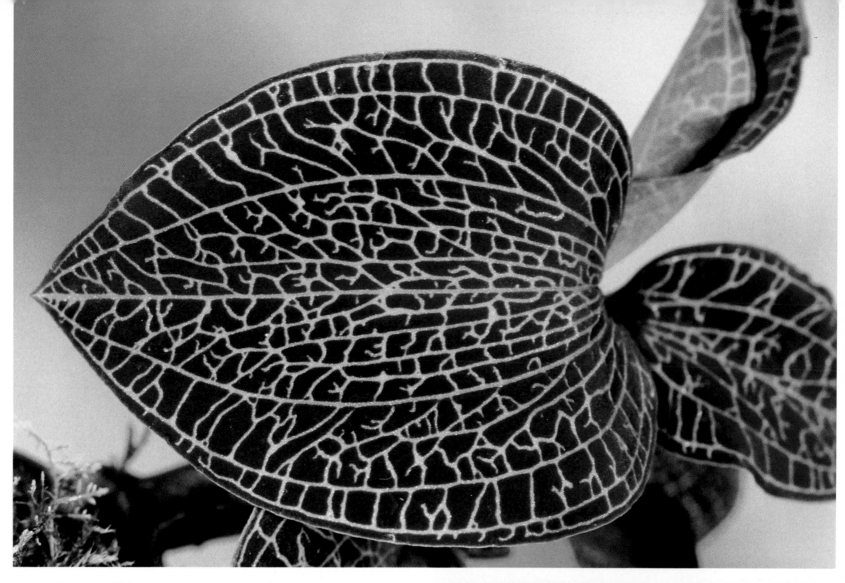

ABOVE: Even orchids can be variegated. This striking vein pattern occurs in *Anoectochilus regalis,* an orchid from the Himalayas.

RIGHT: An attractive variegated cultivar of the English holly *(Ilex aquifolium).*

VARIEGATED LEAVES

BELOW: Many commonly cultivated plants have variegated forms. This variegated cultivar of the rubber plant, *Ficus elastica*, originated in New Orleans in 1925.

BELOW: Begonias show many patterns of variegation. This *Begonia imperialis* was photographed in a garden in England.

VARIEGATED LEAVES

ABOVE AND BELOW: This member of the gesneriad family has brightly colored leaf tips attracting hummingbirds which pollinate the flowers that are hidden under the lower surface of the leaf.

ABOVE: The butterfly orchid, *Oncidium papilio,* from Brazil is an orchid with an unusual mottled variegated pattern.

BELOW: *Episcia cupreata,* a Colombian gesneriad in which the combination of a brightly colored flower and variegated leaves make it an extremely attractive plant.

ABOVE: The bright-red apical leaves of another Brazilian bromeliad. This one is an epiphyte, or air plant, that perches high in the trees.

OPPOSITE PAGE, TOP RIGHT: The center leaves of *Neoregelia carolinae* become scarlet shortly before the plant flowers, which seems to attract the bird pollinators to the flowers of this bromeliad.

OPPOSITE PAGE, BOTTOM RIGHT: This *Alocasia,* an aroid grown in the Amazon region, has a most attractive variegation.

VARIEGATED LEAVES

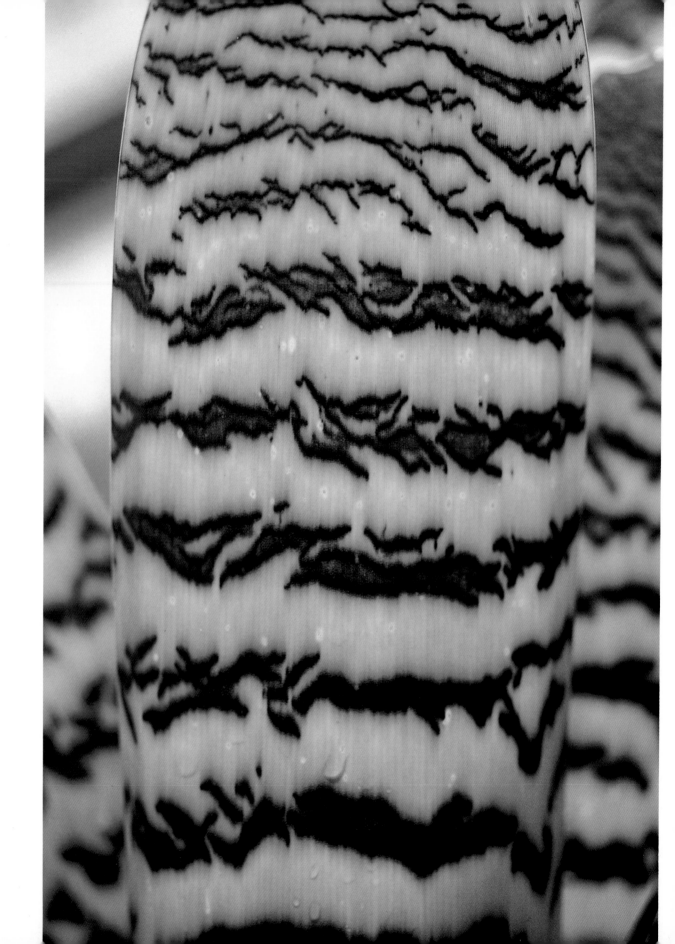

ABOVE: A leaf of *Strobilanthes dyerianus* shows variegation due to the predominance of red pigments rather than the green chlorophyll. This attractive plant from Burma loses its attractive leaf pattern if temperatures drop below 60° F and the leaves turn a dirty gray.

OPPOSITE PAGE: Some bromeliads have an entirely different type of leaf variegation, such as this *Vriesea hieroglyphica* from Brazil, aptly named because its patterns resemble hieroglyphics.

RIGHT: This deep, iridescent blue is an unusual leaf color that occurs in certain species of the fern ally *Selaginella*. It is common in deep-shade forest plants and helps them to absorb the red wavelengths of light.

VARIEGATED LEAVES

Spotty variegation in a *Caladium,* an aroid from Costa Rica. In this
case the spots are of two different colors.

VARIEGATED LEAVES

CHAPTER 8

Floating Leaves

And nearer to the river's trembling edge
There grew broad flag-flowers, purple, pranked with white,
And starry river buds among the sedge,
And floating water-lilies, broad and bright.

PERCY BYSSHE SHELLEY,
"The Question"

A visit to most ponds and lake margins quickly reveals that there are many aquatic plants which have leaves adapted to float. There are a great variety of floating leaves which perform diverse functions for the plant, but the most important is to make it possible for the plant to exist in an aquatic environment and still have leaves exposed to gather light and gases to perform photosynthesis. In some cases the entire plant floats, such as the common duckweeds *(Lemna).* In others the plant is anchored to the lake bottom and just the leaves and flowers float, as in the water lilies.

The queen of all floating leaves must be the Royal water lily, or *Victoria amazonica* (which for many years was incorrectly called *Victoria regia).* The *Victoria* leaves are large floating discs with upturned margins which can be up to eight feet in diameter. Various books and magazines have pictured children floating on these magnificent leaves which will bear up to fifty pounds in weight when they are intact and near to their maximum size. Such depictions of a child sitting peacefully on the leaf would lead one to think the leaves are quite harmless. However, the underside is one of the best examples of a well-protected leaf; it is armed by an abundance of extremely sharp spines over all the ribs, and the underside could certainly not be sat upon! The spines protect these leaves from the many leaf-eating fishes and mammals such as the Amazon sea cow, or manatee.

The underside of the Royal water-lily leaf is a mass of very prominent ribs or veins which radiate from the center and are connected by cross-veins. The girderlike structure that supports this massive floating leaf so impressed the British gardener Joseph Paxton, who was the head gardener of the Duke of Devonshire at Chatsworth House, that it gave him the architectural idea for a greenhouse. He built a conservatory to house the plant based on the leaf structure of *Victoria.* This same design was used as a model for the famous Crystal Palace of the Great Exhibition of 1851 in London, so inspiring is the architecture of these magnificent floating leaves.

The Indians call these leaves the lily-hopper's *(Jacana jacana)* oven *(forno de piacoca).* This combines two facts: that the lily-hopper is the bird most frequently seen flying from leaf to leaf of *Victoria,* and that the leaves look like the ovens in which the natives roast their manioc flour, or farinha. The butterflylike jacana is a very common Amazonian water bird that eats insects from around the leaves of *Victoria.* The birds frequently use the water-lily pad as the base for their primitive nests, which consist of heaps of various water plants piled on top of the large and more robust water-lily leaf.

All water lilies and their relatives have floating leaves that come to the surface from the rhizome on the bottom of the lake or pond in which they grow. The leaves are often attached by a very long petiole so that they reach the surface, unfold, and float. We measured the water depth for some Royal water lilies and found them growing in up to twenty-two feet of water. This means that the leaf petiole must have been at least this length. When water depth reaches twenty-five feet, the *Victoria* lily cannot grow because the distance from the roots to the pads becomes impractical for the plant.

The young leaves are rolled up into a tight and rather small ball with spines facing outward. This protects them well and they are not predated upon by many animals. Once the ball reaches the surface, it unfurls and gradually expands to its maximum size.

The leaves of the temperate water lilies are much smaller, and are not spinous like *Victoria.* However, they can have extremely long petioles. They are also very persistent plants that are difficult to exterminate from a pond once they have taken hold.

Many other pondweeds which are anchored to the bottom of

lakes have floating leaves. However, some have submerged leaves that are able to function underwater. Some plants, such as the aquatic buttercups *(Ranunculus* subgenus *Batrachium),* have both floating and submerged leaves. The two types are completely different in their shape and morphology, and unless one knew that they were attached to the same plant, one would not believe that they could be the same. This is an example of dimorphic leaves or plants which have leaves of two or more shapes. In the case of the water buttercups, the floating leaves are flat and resemble miniature water-lily leaves. The submerged leaves are fine and lacelike and much more appropriate for the life in fast-floating streams.

A tropical plant family in which all 130 species are aquatic is the Podostemonaceae. Most of these plants grow fixed to rocks in fast-flowing streams, whether in the tropics of South America or of Malaysia. Many species have their leaves reduced to small scales. However, one South American species, *Morera fluviatilis,* has leaves that resemble seaweed. The long floating leaves flow downstream from their plant which is firmly attached to the rock. Many of the rapids of the Guianas appear green because of the quantity of this plant and its strange leaves that perform all their functions underwater.

It is fascinating to study the different ways nature has found to achieve flotation of plants. There are many free-floating aquatic plants that have no attachment to the lake bottom. In many, buoyancy is achieved by air-filled, spongy tissue called aerenchyma. Aerenchyma tissue is found in many different aquatic plants. For example, the floating stems of the Amazonian aquatic mimosa, appropriately called *Neptunia,* are surrounded by this tissue and are extremely buoyant. This plant in many respects resembles the true mimosas even to the extent of having sensitive leaves. A member of the evening primrose family, Onagraceae, has aerenchyma on its roots. This plant is called *Ludwigia helminthorrhiza* because of the similarity of the aerenchyma roots to helminthoid worms.

In the temperate regions duckweeds *(Lemna)* are the most familiar floating leaves. They also hold the record for the smallest flowering plant in the world. Members of the genus *Wolffia* in the Lemnaceae family are only one millimeter long. An entire plant is an oval to roundish leaf which floats on ponds or slow-flowing streams. It is not surprising that they are known as water meal, as they form a mealy covering to the ponds in which they grow. *Wolffia* plants have no roots or stems but are just green-colored blobs. The flower, which rarely occurs, develops inside a cavity in the upper surface. As the space is small, it is a simple structure and consists of a single stamen and a single pistil. There are no petals or other structures usually associated with flowers. The duckweeds are believed to be most closely related to the Araceae or the plant family of the skunk cabbage, jack-in-the-pulpit, and arum lily. They have become much reduced as an adaptation to their aquatic life.

A tropical relative of the pondweed is the water lettuce, or *Pistia stratiotes*, an aquatic member of the arum lily family. This floating, cabbagelike plant is common in many tropical lakes and rivers. The leaves form an extremely symmetrical pattern.

In the tropics, the water hyacinth *(Eichhornia crassipes)* is the best-known example of a floating plant. In this case the plants are made buoyant by air-filled petiole bases rather than by aerenchyma. The water hyacinth has an attractive flower, and so it is not surprising that it was introduced to a horticultural exhibition in Louisiana in 1864. From there it escaped and has become one of the greatest aquatic weed problems in the Gulf states and Florida. Similarly it was introduced to both the Nile and the Congo in Africa where it is out of control. In India it is a tremendous problem. However, in the Amazon where it is native it does not get out of control. Its natural predators keep it from becoming too large a population, and large amounts are also flushed out to sea each year by the rising waters of the flood season. It is common to see huge mats of water hyacinth floating down the Amazon and its tributaries. The most recent research has been to find ways in which its enormous productivity can be put to use. Water hyacinth is being successfully used to generate methane in India, to mix with cattle fodder in Mato Grosso, Brazil, and for the treatment of sewage in the southern United States. Many aquatic plants have the property of being able to reproduce and grow extremely rapidly and so this provides biomass that can be rather easily harvested if appropriate uses are found. The aquatic fern *Salvinia auriculata* is also used for methane because of its productivity.

The *Salvinia* water fern and the water lettuce invaded Lake Kariba on the Zambezi River shortly after the sluice gates were closed and the dam began to fill. The water fern *(Salvinia auriculata)* severely interfered with the many uses proposed for the lake behind the Kariba dam. Eventually, at considerable expense, a barrier was erected to keep the aquatic plants away from the inlets of the turbines.

Floating plants belong to many different types of plants. Some of the most interesting are the aquatic ferns. They do not look like terrestrial ferns at first sight since they have had to change their morphology to one appropriate to the aquatic environment. *Salvinia* has a flat, platelike blade that resembles miniature water-lily leaves. It is one of the most abundant and productive of tropical aquatic plants. *Marsilea* is quite different and has fronds which closely resemble the shamrock. However, they unfurl from a characteristic fiddlehead shape which gives away the relationship of this plant. *Azolla* is a useful fern because in addition to its high productivity it lives in symbiosis with nitrogen-fixing bacteria. The Japanese are careful to infect their rice paddies with *Azolla* to help replace the nitrogen, just as legumes are used in pastures.

There are even floating liverworts *(Ricciocarpus natans)* which represent one of the simplest kind of plants.

ABOVE: The floating leaves of an Amazonian water lily *(Nymphaea rudgeana).*

The variety of aquatic leaves, and the different ways in which so many different kinds of plants have become adapted to the aquatic environment, show the versatility of the process of adaptation to an environment.

OPPOSITE PAGE: *Victoria amazonica,* the royal water lily, growing near Manaus, Brazil. With their upturned margins, these floating saucers can bear considerable weight.

RIGHT: A young leaf of the royal water lily, half unfolded. The leaf begins as a spiny ball which gradually unrolls and flattens out.

BELOW: Water lily leaves in Sri Lanka.

RIGHT: Kjell Sandved photographing aquatic plants in Virginia, not always the pleasantest job!

BELOW: Kjell Sandved photographing the royal water lily.

LEFT: An upturned leaf of the royal water lily, showing the conspicuous ribbed veins that inspired the design of the Crystal Palace in London.

BELOW: The water key, or *Hydrocleys commersonii,* is an attractive aquatic from ponds in Brazil.

This *Morera* belongs to the Podostemonaceae, a plant family that grows only on the rocks of rapids in fast-flowing rivers.

BELOW: A mass of *Azolla,* one of the aquatic ferns from Colombia.

FLOATING LEAVES

ABOVE: *Pistia,* the water lettuce, with its cabbagelike leaves is common around the tropics. A relative of the arum lily, it is shown here in Amazonian Brazil.

LEFT: A young leaf of the royal water lily, almost completely unrolled.

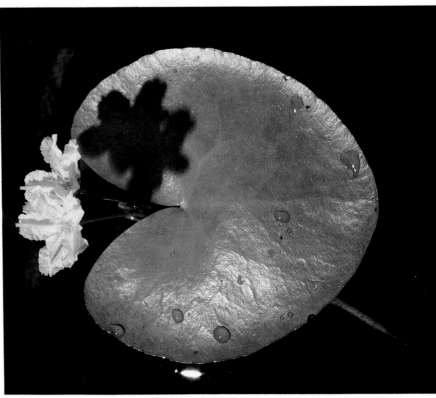

ABOVE: This *Limnanthemum cristatum,* photographed in Sri Lanka, is an aquatic relative of the gentian.

LEFT: *Azolla* is also important for rice paddies because of its associated nitrogen-fixing bacteria.

BELOW: The leaf undersurface of some water lilies is purple as in this tropical cultivated form of *Nymphaea* Albert Grenberg.

RIGHT: Variegated water lily leaves such as this *Nymphaea* Director Moore are popular in cultivation.

BELOW: The leaves of the *Salvinia* fern are small but the mass of plants often clog up ponds and rice paddies.

ABOVE: *Marsilea* is an aquatic fern with clover-shaped leaves. This *M. mutica* from New Caledonia has four leaflets. Others are trifoliate like the shamrock.

Author Ghillean Prance demonstrates the underside of a leaf of *Victoria amazonica* water lily. His study of the pollination of that lily involved much waist-deep wading in Amazon lakes.

FLOATING LEAVES

CHAPTER 9

Succulent Leaves

Succulent is the term given to any fleshy plant belonging to a large number of different plant families. Examples of succulent plants include houseleek, stonecrops, various Euphorbias, agave, and yucca. The cacti are succulent, but the term is more often given to fleshy plants other than cacti. Plants have become succulent as an adaptation to arid and semiarid regions where water conservation is of primary importance to the plant. It is evolution's adaptation to the extremes of heat and aridity of desert regions of the world.

Succulent leaves are an ideal leaf form for a dry region because their thick shape combines a small surface area with maximum contents. The nearer to a globe the leaf shape is, the more efficient the leaf. In addition to reduced surface area, succulent leaves usually have a thick cuticle or outer surface which reduces evaporation from the inner layers whose fleshy tissues store water for the plant.

Many succulents are familiar to horticulturists because of the unusual growth forms they exhibit. Among the most bizarre are the stone plants *(Lithops),* which are native to South Africa and are sold by many plant sellers. The leaves of the stone plants exactly resemble pebbles in both color and texture. Since they grow in the desert among pebbles they are so well disguised as stones that they are overlooked by browsing animals, of which there are many in South Africa.

The stone plants consist of two large succulent leaves which are close together and taper from the top to form a cone-shaped body, the apex of which is attached to the underground stem of the plant. Only about an inch of the broad end of the cone shows above the ground. There are many species of stone plants that closely resemble the different rock and pebble types of the South African desert on which they grow. This remarkable pair of leaves can look like quartz pebbles, a chunk of iron ore, or even weathered limestone. Their disguise is given away only for a brief period when they flower. The brightly colored, conspicuous flowers spring up between the leaves to attract pollinators. It is often only then that even the most avid collector can find these plants, which are among the most perfectly camouflaged of all plants.

A succulent group that are highly popular as garden and especially rock-garden herbs are the stonecrops, which belong to the plant family Crassulaceae. The large South African genus *Crassula* has many species in the same habitats as the stone plants. However, the Sedums may be better known in North America since they are abundant in the southwestern United States. The various stonecrops are commonly known by such names as orpine, hen-and-chickens, frogplant, and live-forever. The other commonly cultivated genus of the stonecrop family is *Kalanchoë*. The houseleek *(Sempervivum tectorum)* is well known in Ireland and Britain because it frequently grows on moss-covered stone roofs. These are left growing not only for their beauty, but also because they are said to bring good luck to the occupants of the house.

Another succulent from South Africa, the aloe *(Aloe)*, is steeped in legend and history. The aloes belong to the lily family and resemble the century plants *(Agave)* in their large basal rosette of lancelike leaves. The aloes were transported by humans from Africa around the Mediterranean into Asia. It eventually became a sacred plant to the Muslims, who hang aloe leaves over their doors after a pilgrimage to Mecca to show that they have made the journey. The aloe leaves also contain the purgative aloin. They were known as useful medicinal plants to such classical writers as Dioscorides and Pliny the Elder. The aloes are extensively cultivated in the West Indies and can be seen in abundance on the islands of Curaçao and Jamaica. Today the aloe is used in medicated soaps and creams.

TOP RIGHT: The leaves of a prickly pear, *Opuntia.*

BOTTOM RIGHT: An orchid with succulent leaves *(Epidendrum impiricatum).*

Leaves of the South African succulent *Crassula hottentotta.*

OPPOSITE PAGE, LEFT: The swollen succulent leaf base of this *Bulbophyllum* orchid serves as a water-storage organ.

OPPOSITE PAGE, RIGHT: The dainty, succulent leaves of the fern, *Drymoglossum heterophyllum* from Sri Lanka.

RIGHT: A succulent *Kalanchoë* from Madagascar.

BELOW: This cactuslike plant is a succulent *Euphorbia* (*E. lactea*) from India.

SUCCULENT LEAVES

LEFT: *Euphorbia obesa* is well named, with its swollen, succulent, cactuslike stem. It is a native of the South African desert where no cacti grow.

BELOW: The two peglike leaves of a stone plant *(Lithops).*

LEFT: A variety of stone plants, showing adaptation to camouflage patterns among different rocks.

SUCCULENT LEAVES

ABOVE AND BELOW: The stone plants lose their disguise when they bloom with colorful flowers.

RIGHT: The cactus is the characteristic succulent of New World deserts. In most cacti, the leaves are reduced to spines and the stem is green and performs the photosynthesis.

CHAPTER 10

Poisons and Prickles: Leaves That Defend Their Plant

Tender-handed stroke a nettle,
And it stings you for your pains;
Grasp it like a man of mettle,
And it soft as silk remains.

AARON HILL
"Verses Written on Window"

So far we have considered many aspects of leaves that are useful and pleasing to humans. However, there are other types of leaves which we do not find so pleasant but which perform a vital function for the plant to which they belong—that of defense from predators. These are the leaves that sting like the nettle, are prickly like holly, cause allergies like poison ivy, or are poisonous like those of the commonly used houseplant *Dieffenbachia*.

During the course of evolution there has been a constant battle between leaf-eating animals and the plants which need to retain their leaves to capture energy. There are many herbivorous animals in the world, varying from the large browsers like elephants and giraffes to the small insects that are discussed in Chapter 19. These phytophagous, or leaf-eating, animals can destroy whole plants and so the process of natural selection has favored the survival of leaves that are more prickly or more poisonous. For the survival of many species of plants it has been necessary to develop many characteristics which are noxious to us but are vital for the plant.

Perhaps the most unpleasant and best known are leaves that sting when touched. These leaves inject a poison that can cause considerable pain. The nettles are the best known and almost universal example of stinging leaves. They vary from the common stinging nettle (Urtica dioica) to tropical trees of the Amazon and the East Indies. The worst of all, which should be avoided at all costs, is the devil's leaf nettle of Malesia and northern Australia which frequently causes pain for up to one year after the leaf is touched! It is dreaded by plant collectors who work in the region and have to handle many plants. Another plant family with some species that have stinging leaves are the spurges, or Euphorbiaceae.

Nettles sting through the bristles or hairs that cover their leaves. These hairs are hollow and have fragile, sealed tips. At the other end of their base, inside the leaf epidermis, there is a bulb which is filled with poison and fits neatly into a socketlike structure formed by the surrounding cells. When the hairs are touched, the pressure fractures the tips of the hairs and drives them into the skin like a series of small hypodermic needles. The same pressure also pushes the base down into the socket and thereby forces the poison through the tip of the needle, injecting the victim with poison. In the case of the common nettle this is felt for only a few minutes, but many other species are far worse. The sting is an effective defense against many predators.

Other leaves are defended by nontoxic spines. In this case the margins are often bordered by a series of prickles. The holly is a familiar example as are many species of thistle. The spines on leaves are formed at the margins generally by hardened and sharp extensions of the endings of the primary leaf veins. In some cases it is the leaf hairs that have become hard and thornlike. The thorns on the leaf veins of roses are well known to gardeners.

The extreme is found in the cacti where there are generally no leaves. Instead, the green succulent stem is covered with spines which are in fact formed from reduced vestigial leaves. There are very few cacti with true leaves; in most species they have been reduced to what are often extremely vicious spines. The loss of leaves in these desert plants is useful as it avoids loss of water, and the plant is defended by the spines that remain.

The terminal leaf spines of the giant agave leaves of Mexico can be detached together with a natural thread of fibers that remain attached to the spines. This is used by the natives as an already threaded needle to sew up sacks and work clothing.

Some leaves which look perfectly normal to the eye have a hidden defense, that of poison in the leaf. The poisons or bitter tastes obviously discourage animals from browsing. Leaves that are unpleasant-tasting or poisonous are often ignored by browsing animals, which explains the increase in docks (Rumex) and ragwort (Senecio jacobaea) in the pastures of Britain. However, animals do not always know when to reject poisonous leaves. Horses will eat any available leaves of yew (Taxus baccata) with great relish, although only a few mouthfuls are fatal to them.

Several of our common houseplants have poisonous leaves. Those that most frequently cause trouble to children and pets are various members of the skunk cabbage family, or Araceae. The Dieffenbachia, for example, is one of the commonest houseplants, but it is also dangerous. The leaves contain thousands of fine, needlelike crystals of calcium oxalate which pierce the roof of the mouth when eaten. In addition they have a poison that causes swelling. Together with the mechanical effect and the poison, the swelling can quickly become so grave that it causes asphyxiation. Medical help is required immediately for someone who has eaten a Dieffenbachia leaf. It is well named dumbcane!

One of the most poisonous of all leaves, and one that features in history several times, is the poison hemlock (Conium maculatum), a native plant of Europe that is unfortunately naturalized along the waysides of the United States. This herb with parsleylike leaves belongs to the parsley family and some people have had the misfortune to mistake it for parsley. The volatile alkaloid coniine, found in the plant, is fatal even in small doses. The ancient Greeks used poison hemlock to administer the death penalty to prisoners, the most notable of whom was the philosopher Socrates. The condemned prisoner was allowed to swallow the fatal cup of hemlock. This poisonous herb should not be confused with the hemlock tree (Tsuga), the leaves of which are not poisonous.

Another use of poisonous leaves is that of the Amazon Indians and other native groups around the world who have discovered which leaves are good as fish poisons, or barbasco. For example, the Maku Indians of Amazonian Colombia and Brazil use the leaves of two plants of the spurge family, Euphorbia cotinifolia and Phyllanthus brasiliensis. A bundle of leaves of one of these species is collected and then placed on a log bridge over a small stream. The Indians beat the leaves with a stick to break them up and allow the juices to drip into the stream. At the same time they are careful to keep their eyes closed to avoid the juices and latex splashing into their eyes. The women of the tribe gather downstream from the leaf beaters and in a few minutes the fish in a 200-yard area below the poison are stunned. They float to the surface and are easily collected in palm-leaf baskets. The action of the poison affects the fishes' gills and they are asphyxiated rather than poisoned, and therefore are edible after this process. Other tribes of Indians use roots and stems of various vines, but the leaves of these two members of the spurge family are as effective as any other fish poison we have seen.

The chemical substances in leaves are diverse and interesting, which is why leaves have so many uses as flavors and medicines, but they can also be dangerous. Some of the substances that repel animals have an extremely toxic, allergenic effect on humans. The poison ivy *(Rhus toxicodendron)* and poison sumac *(Rhus vernix)* are two of the best known and most drastic. Many people dread walking in the forests of the northeastern United States for fear of brushing into a leaf of poison ivy, which can cause a severe rash. The Europeans are fortunate because these two plants do not grow on their continent.

Visitors to the beautiful beaches of Central America and some Caribbean islands have often sheltered under the shade of a common seaside plant, the mancineel *(Hippomane mancinella)*, only to break out in a bad rash from the poison which drips from the leaves of that tree. Those people who have tasted its sweet-smelling fruit are in more serious trouble, as a few mouthfuls of the fruit can be fatal.

Other leaves are poisonous in a different way. The chemicals that they contain inhibit the growth of other plants. This phenomenon, called allelopathy, is caused by the rain washing chemical repellents off the leaves into the soil. The soil becomes so toxic that other plants cannot grow. This is why there are so few other plants under a *Eucalyptus* plantation. The American brittlewood is a good example of an allelopathic plant. It excludes other species so that they do not grow nearby and compete for the precious soil nutrients and water.

Poisons and prickles may seem annoying to us, but when we look at the reason for their presence on or in the leaf we see again how ingenious nature is in preserving and protecting the diversity of life.

TOP RIGHT: The leaves of this sea holly *(Eryngium maritimum)* have their margins drawn out into prickles.

BOTTOM RIGHT: Many members of the jack-in-the-pulpit family, Araceae, are poisonous because of the thin, needlelike oxalate crystals.

BELOW: Leaves of the castor bean plant *(Ricinus communis)* in East Africa. It is good to be able to recognize these in the tropics since it is one of the most poisonous plants.

LEAVES THAT DEFEND THEIR PLANT

The Andean plant *Coriaria* is a danger to cattle because it often appears in pastures and has extremely toxic leaves.

BELOW: Maku Indians of Brazil preparing their fish poison by beating the juices out of the leaves of *Euphorbia cotinifolia* into a small stream.

ABOVE: The commonly cultivated ornamental vine *Allamanda cathartica* is in fact a poisonous plant.

Leaves of Prey: Carnivorous Plants

This plant, commonly called Venus' flytrap, from the rapidity and force of its movements, is one of the most wonderful in the world.

CHARLES DARWIN,
Insectivorous Plants

Some of the most bizarre leaves are those adapted to catch insects as a source of nutrition for the plants to which they belong. As long ago as 1875 Charles Darwin wrote a book about insectivorous plants that described many in great detail. More recently, however, they have come to be known as carnivorous plants because some of them also digest small animals such as frogs, fishes, and mice. In all cases it is modifications of the leaves that enable the plant to trap its animal food.

Most plants obtain their nutrition directly from the gases in the air and the minerals and water in the soil. Carnivorous plants are unique in that they also feed on animals which they capture and digest. Carnivorous plants are common in acid bogs where there is little nitrogen. The insect material that they digest is rich in nitrogen, so carnivory in plants is an adaptation to survival in nutrient-poor habitats. Once they have trapped an animal, the carnivorous plants secrete enzymes which digest the animal in an acid environment that inhibits putrefaction.

Carnivorous plants are generally divided into two groups based on the method in which they capture their prey: active trappers and passive trappers. Active trappers capture their prey by movement of a part when it is triggered; passive trappers just wait for their prey to become stuck to the plant or trapped inside a hollow structure.

The best-known active trapper is the Venus' flytrap (Dionaea muscipula). It is a native of the coastal plains of North and South Carolina where it is rather rare. It is, however, comparatively easy to cultivate and is cultivated around the world as a curiosity. Since it can be grown from seed, the cultivation does not necessarily destroy the wild populations. The Venus' flytrap is frequently available for sale in supermarkets and florist shops. The leaf, which has a flattened stalk, is roundish and divided into two symmetrical halves by the midvein. On the open leaf there are masses of minute, short-stalked glands that will later secrete the plant's digestive juices. Clearly visible are three stiff hairs that protrude from the leaf blade and are the triggers that set off the trap. When an insect touches the trigger hairs twice, the two halves of the leaf close tightly together, moving inward from the hinged base just like a steel leg trap for an animal. The unfortunate insect, usually an ant rather than a fly, is caught firmly. The glands secrete enzymes and the leaf begins to function as a stomach, digesting the insect. After a week the insect is digested and the leaf reopens, ready to trap a new victim. The trigger hairs only work if one hair is touched twice within a short interval or two hairs once each. This probably avoids many false alarms.

Recently, scientists Alan Bennett of Cornell University and Stephen Williams of Lebanon Valley College have shown that it is an acid flux that triggers the Venus' flytrap to close so quickly. The cells of the opening or closing traps acidify their own walls by releasing hydrogen ions. The drop in pH of the cell walls causes extremely rapid growth of the cells of the outer surface of the leaf. During the ten hours of reopening, the inner surface slowly expands. This is a different mechanism from the turgor change that causes the sensitive leaves of mimosa to close, as described in Chapter 18.

The bladderwort (Utricularia) is a worldwide genus of more than 150 species of aquatic plants. They have extremely modified leaves that are generally underwater and form small, elastic-walled bladders, which give the plant its popular name. The entrance to the bladder also has trigger hairs. When the triggers are touched, the prey, such as small crustaceans, are actually sucked into the bladder by a current of water produced by the bladder walls springing apart, like air entering a vacuum in a soft-walled plastic bottle. Bladderworts eat small aquatic animals including mosquito larvae,

which makes some of them important for the control of mosquitos in the tropics. The insect is digested in the bladder and the trap resets when the walls flatten again.

Passive traps function in two ways: through secreting a sticky substance that traps insects like flypaper, or by enticing prey to enter a hollow leaf that is difficult to escape from.

The sundews (Drosera species) are the most widespread and commonest carnivorous plants. Their many species are found from the northern bogs to the humid tropics. They are rather small, inconspicuous plants which can be overlooked easily by the uninitiated. They produce small whorls of spoon-shaped or spatulalike leaves. The leaf blades are covered by thousands of glandular hairs that secrete tiny drops of sticky glue. Any small insect that lands on the leaf is stuck there. Some of the hairs, or tentacles, as they are often called, secrete the digestive juices. The tentacles bend over the insect and push it toward the center, where the digestive juices are produced, and the insect remains bound up with tentacles until it is completely digested.

The butterworts (Pinguicula) are relatives of the bladderworts. Their trap is not made of bladders but is of the flypaper variety, with a sticky substance secreted on the leaves. The juices of the bladderwort are also antiseptic; Alpine shepherds have known for centuries that they are useful to cure udder sores on cows.

The pitcher plants belong to the plant family Sarraceniaceae, which is an American group of bog plants. They catch insects by a "pitfall" rather than by active movement. The traps are highly specialized, modified, hollow, cylindrical leaves. The flap at the mouth is often colorful like a flower and secretes nectar. The leaves with their nectar and color simulate and mimic flowers, which attract insects. The insects arrive at the fake flower, land, and lose their balance on the slippery interior of the pitcher mouth. They fall downward through the throat of the pitcher, which has an array of downward-pointing hairs. The hairs allow the insects to move down but not to fly back up. The interior is a slippery chute that precipitates the insect down to the bottom of the pitcher where there is a liquid in which the insect lands. This foul-smelling fluid first stupefies the insect and then begins the digestive process. There are specialized epidermal cells in the base of the pitcher that are capable of absorbing the nutrients as the insects are digested.

There are many different pitcher plants. Although they look different they all function in much the same way. The commonest in North America is the purple pitcher plant (Sarracenia purpurea), which occurs from Florida to as far north as Labrador. The California pitcher plant (Darlingtonia californica) has a translucent window in the pitcher. Insects will try to escape through this closed window instead of the opening through which they entered and will become exhausted and fall into the liquid below. Darlingtonia does not secrete enzymes to digest its prey, but depends on the action of bacteria. The South American pitcher plant *Heliamphora* grows only on the top of some of the table mountains of the Guayana Highlands of Venezuela, the "lost world" of novelist Conan Doyle.

How can a generally flat leaf blade become a hollow tube as it has in the pitchers? It is generally believed that over many years and generations the leaf margins have fused and modified a flat leaf into a cylinder.

Perhaps the most bizarre of all pitfall carnivorous plants is *Nepenthes*, a tropical Asiatic genus of the family Nepenthaceae. In *Nepenthes* some of the leaves are modified into pitchers which are borne on the ends of extremely long stalks. The upright pitchers dangle down below the plant and attract insects similarly to the pitcher plants. However, the pitchers of some species are so large (large enough to hold a rat!) that frequently small animals such as frogs and lizards end up as victims. The *Nepenthes* grow as air plants in areas of particularly poor white-sand soils in tropical Asia.

Carnivorous plants have diverse ways of adapting their leaves to attract and catch their food. Leaves that are sticky flypapers, hollow pits with a digestive fluid at the base, spring traps, and underwater suction pumps are all part of the varied leaf structure of the plant kingdom.

The sticky leaves of these *Drosera* have numerous tentacles that wrap around a captive insect.

LEFT AND OPPOSITE PAGE, RIGHT: Insects stuck on a leaf of *Drosera capensis* from South Africa.

BELOW AND OPPOSITE PAGE, LEFT: The most common North American pitcher plant, *Sarracenia purpurea*, lures insects into the pitchers.

LEAVES OF PREY

LEAVES OF PREY

Pitchers of Nepenthes, *the tropical Asian pitcher plants common in the jungles of Borneo.*

Nepenthes tentaculata at Kota Kinabalu, Sabah.

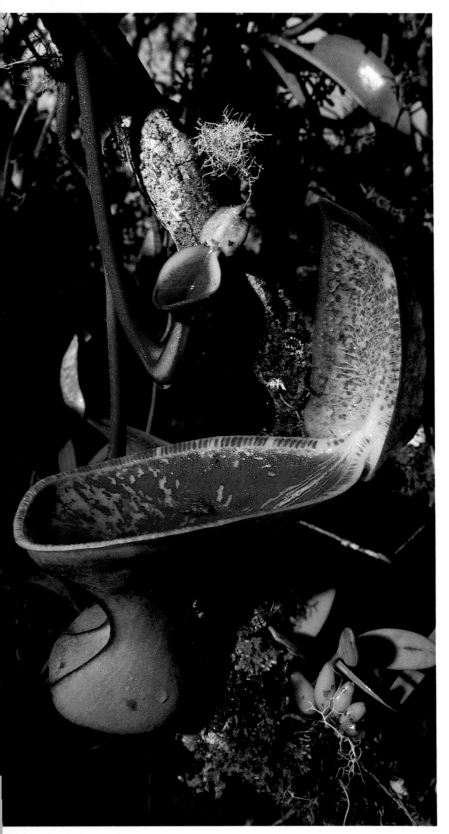

Nepenthes lowii at Kota Kinabalu, Sabah.

Nepenthes gracilis at Kota Kinabalu, Sabah.

Nepenthes gracilis at Kota Kinabalu, Sabah.

Nepenthes gymnamphora on Sumatra.

A Thomisidae: Misumenops spider in the dissected pitcher of *Nepenthes gymnamphora* on Sumatra.

BELOW: *Darlingtonia californica,* the California pitcher plant. The mottled surface of the pitcher functions as windows to let in light and confuse the trapped insects.

RIGHT: *Cephalotus follicularis* is an Australian pitcher plant.

Bromeliad water tanks are formed at the leaf bases. Many organisms live in the water. In a few bromeliads, insects are trapped and digested.

OPPOSITE PAGE, TOP: A species of *Aechmea* in Brazil.

BELOW: *Neoregelia carolinae,* the cup of flame bromeliad of Brazil.

ABOVE: The whole plant.

The Venus' flytrap, Dionaea muscipula.

BELOW: The leaves are often red to attract insects.

ABOVE: A single leaf, showing the trigger hairs. In this open leaf the trap is set ready to spring shut when the trigger hairs are touched.

BELOW: The leaves are open and ready for insects.

CHAPTER 12

Leaves as Homes

Go to the ant, thou sluggard; consider her ways, and be wise.
PROVERBS VI: 6

Leaves have become adapted in many different ways to perform multiple functions for plants. Some of the most interesting of all leaves are those that have become adapted to house various insects, especially ants. As is true in most biological interactions, there is mutual benefit: not only does the plant house the insects, but in return the insects perform a service for the plant.

Ant-inhabited plants are called myrmecophytes, and the cavities in which the ants live are called myrmecodomatia (derived from the Greek word for ant, *myrmex,* and the Latin for house, *domus*). Ants inhabit many plants. In some they live in the hollow stems, for example, in the *Cecropia* tree that is characteristic of all secondary neotropical forest, and is inhabited by *Azteca* fire ants. Here, however, we are concerned only with leaves that are homes for ants.

There are a number of species in the neotropical forest that have ant pouches at the base of their leaf blades. These paired pouches consist of a chamber with a narrow opening usually onto the underside of the leaf or petiole. Species that have this type of pouch usually have a dense mass of stiff, or hispid, hairs covering the leaves, ant pouches, and stems of the plant. This type of adaptation has evolved several times in unrelated groups of plants, showing that it is of considerable selective advantage. These pouches are most common in the melastome family, for example, in the genera *Clidemia, Conostegia, Henriettella, Maieta,* and *Tococa.* They also occur in *Duroia,* a member of the coffee family (Rubiaceae), in *Cordia,* a member of the borage family (Boraginaceae), and in *Hirtella,* a member of the cocoa plum family (Chrysobalanaceae). In the African forests ant pouches occur in the leaves of two genera of the cacao family (Sterculiaceae), in *Scaphopetalum* and in *Cola,* the genus that yields the cola beans used in cola drinks.

Some ant cavities, such as those of the melastomes and cola, develop through a swelling of the leaf undersurface so that they are actually inflated parts of the lower leaf surface. In the case of *Duroia* and *Hirtella,* the pouches are formed from the curling under of the leaf margin on each side of the leaf base, near the junction with the petiole. Pouches are formed from the petiole in three species of Central American *Piper,* in the black pepper family. In this case, petiolar sheaths fold over and form a tube on the top of each petiole. All these different methods form similar structures whose function is to house the ants.

Since these structures have evolved repeatedly, they must be beneficial to the plants and not merely houses for the ants. Ant cavities benefit the plant in two possible ways, and in some cases both probably occur from the same interaction. First, ants in leaf cavities of a plant help to defend it from attack by leaf-eating insects. The ants are also effective predators of mites and insect eggs and this helps to reduce predation of the plant. Second, the ants leave detritus in the cavities. This comes from nest-construction material and feces, and in some cases the plants can absorb nutrients from the detritus in the ant cavities.

The types of ants that inhabit leaf pouches belong to the family Myrmicinae in the genera *Pheidole, Crematogaster,* and *Allomerus,* the Dolichoderinae genus *Azteca,* and the Formicinae genus *Myrmelachiste.*

One of the most unusual of all leaf types is found in the genus *Dischidia* of the Asiatic and Pacific tropics and belongs to the milkweed family (Asclepiadaceae). This is a genus of some eighty different species of epiphytes, or air plants, that are perched in the crowns of trees. About half of the species of *Dischidia* are adapted to house or shelter ants in modified leaves.

One of the group of *Dischidia* species has dome-shaped leaves with their edges pressed tightly against the bark of the host tree. A second group of species has some of the leaves modified into cylindrical, flask-shaped structures, and a third group of species has flasklike leaves with a second small chamber within the

outer one. It is easy to see how the flask-shaped leaves could have evolved from the domed ones by the turning in and fusion of the leaf edges.

The dome-shaped leaves have roots arising near their stalk and entering into the space underneath. Roots also enter into the flask leaves, but not into the inner chamber. The cavities of all these types of leaves are inhabited by the scavenging ant *Iridomyrmex.* These ants bring debris into the cavities, and scientists have observed that the greater the quantity of leaves, the greater the amount of roots produced by the plants, since the roots absorb nutrients from the debris and fecal material of the ants. The nutrients from the ant detritus are important for an air plant perched high in the trees where there is no soil. The ants also construct sheltered carton (papier-mâchélike) pathways over the external roots and along the stems of *Dischidia.* In return, the cavities in the leaves of the plant provide an excellent home for the ants. The ants also feed on the oil bodies of the seeds of *Dischidia* and at the same time move around or disperse the seeds.

The bromeliad or pineapple family is one of the largest groups of epiphytic plants in the American tropics. Most bromeliads have leaves in a basal whorl from which the flowering stalk eventually emerges. In many cases the leaves are open and form a reservoir where rainwater can accumulate. These bromeliad tanks hold their own small world. A glance under a microscope at the water from these plants shows thousands of microorganisms swimming around. There is even a species of the carnivorous bladderwort (see the preceding chapter) that lives in bromeliad water tanks. The plants have a series of stalked scales on the inside of their leaves. It has been shown with use of radioactive tracers that nutrients are absorbed by the plants directly from the water tanks.

A few bromeliads have adapted a different strategy to obtain nutrition and have completely dry, modified tanks. The bulbous *Tillandsia (T. bulbosa),* for example, has the leaves tightly constricted against the central flower stalk so that water cannot enter the spaces between the leaf bases. The leaf blades are rolled in such a way that water is not channeled along them toward the center as it is in many tank bromeliads. Although the top of the tank is tightly closed, the bottoms of the leaves are not so tightly pressed onto each other. This allows spaces between the leaf blades where ants can enter. The inner surfaces of these ant homes have large scales that absorb nutrients from the ant detritus, and it has been proven that the plants take up calcium through their leaf sheaths. These bromeliad ant homes are inhabited by *Crematogaster* ants.

Other leaves do not house ants, but have developed ant lures. They attract ants to leaves where they stay to feed. The lures are glands that secrete nectar, a sugar solution similar to the nectar of flowers which attracts pollinators. There are many plants with these glands on their leaves. Sugar-producing glands that occur outside the flowers for purposes other than pollination are known as extrafloral nectaries.

One of the most conspicuous of all the extrafloral nectaries occurs on the leaves of most species of the large tropical genus *Inga*. Since *Inga* is a legume, it has a compound leaf with a central rachis and many pairs of lateral leaflets. Between each leaflet pair on the upper surface of the rachis are cuplike nectaries that secrete a sugar solution which attracts ants. The ants feed on the nectar and at the same time defend the plant from leaf-eating insects. It has been shown that when the access of ants to the leaves is blocked there is considerably more leaf predation.

Extrafloral nectaries of this type occur in many other plants besides the Ingas. The attractive tropical relative of the ginger called *Costus* has nectaries on the colorful flower leaves or bracts. The nectaries of the *Costus* bracts are tended by *Wasmannia* and *Camponotus* ants. Scientist David Schenske showed that when he prevented ants from tending the nectaries of *Costus woodsonii* from Panama the production of seeds was reduced by two-thirds because of predation by fly larvae. In this case the nectaries on the flower leaves function to protect the developing seeds as well as the leaves themselves.

Many members of the catalpa family, Bignoniaceae, also have extrafloral nectaries on the bracts, including one of the few North American representatives of this family, the trumpet creeper *(Campsis radicans).* In this case the nectaries are tended by small ants of the genera *Formica*, *Lasius alienus americanus,* and *Crematogaster lineolata.* The elder and various wild cherries are other temperate region plants with extrafloral nectaries to attract defender ants.

Perhaps the most bizarre of all ant leaves are those of the bull-horn acacia *(Acacia cornigera),* where the stipules have become modified into a pair of hollow spines that resemble a bull's horns. These thorns, at the base of each leaf, are inhabited by an extremely aggressive ant of the genus *Pseudomyrmex.* These fierce, stinging ants cut an entrance hole into the thorns, eat the sweet-tasting pith to make a large cavity, and then have an ideal, well-protected home. In addition to providing a home for the ant, the acacia also feeds its protectors from a row of cuplike nectaries located at the base of each leaf. However, to ensure that the ants patrol the leaves, the acacia plant also produces small fatty globules at the apex of each leaflet, called Beltian bodies after the English naturalist Thomas Belt (1832–1878), who first described them. The ants forage around the leaflet tips to eat the maturing Beltian bodies and consequently continuously guard the leaves. The acacia ants are extremely aggressive; it is thought that they effectively deter larger browsing animals as well as insects from entering their host plant. By combining its thorns and ants the acacia has developed one of the best defense mechanisms of any plant. Daniel Janzen has shown that plants from which the ants

have been removed are attacked more by predators. Since the acacia has invested all its efforts in ant-defense mechanisms and the production of both extrafloral nectaries and Beltian bodies, it does not have chemical defenses and its leaves are highly palatable to most predators. Yet in nature they are seldom severely attacked because of the efficacy of the ant protection.

We often regard insects, and especially the highly destructive leaf-cutting ants of the tropics, as only predators of leaves. However, as we see here, there are many plants which have made good use of the abundance of insects around them and have developed a symbiosis with ants through modifications of their leaves or other organs.

ABOVE: The characteristic palmate leaf of the *Cecropia,* whose stem is inhabited by fierce fire ants that afford protection to the tree.

BELOW: At the base of the leaf petiole, near its junction with the stem, each *Cecropia* leaf has a pad that produces fatty bodies called Muellerian bodies. These serve as food for the ants that inhabit the plant, but here a wasp is robbing the ants' food.

The leaves of various species of South American melastomes have inflated ant cavities at their base. The ants that live in these pouches protect the leaves from predation by other insects.

LEAVES AS HOMES

TOP LEFT: Ants feeding on scale insects on the leaf of a plant near Manaus, Brazil. The ants, which feed on the honeydew produced by the insects, also help protect the leaf from predators.

BOTTOM, LEFT: The young leaf of a species of *Inga* from Colombia. The cups along the central stalk between each leaflet pair are a nectary which feeds its protector ants. The nectaries develop first before the leaflets expand so that the young leaves are well protected when they are soft and tender and most in need of defenders.

ABOVE: The flower of a species of *Costus* from Amazonian Brazil. The bracts that protect the flower secrete a sugar solution which is fed upon by ants, whose presence greatly reduces seed predation by fly larvae.

ABOVE: A mature leaf of an *Inga* from Costa Rica with an ant feeding on the extrafloral nectary.

TOP RIGHT: The nest of a weaver ant *(Oecophylla longinoda)* from Ghana.

MIDDLE RIGHT: Ants at the extrafloral nectaries of a *Strychnos* vine in the Amazon forest. The sugar produced by the nectaries feeds the ants, which in return protect the leaves from other predators.

BOTTOM RIGHT: The petiole base of a *Cecropia* leaf from Chocó, Colombia, showing the fatty Muellerian bodies that provide food for the protector ants that inhabit the tree.

BELOW: Not all uses of leaves as homes are beneficial. Here an Amazonian rainforest spider has made its nest by rolling up a leaf.

BELOW: An ant at the studlike nectaries on the petiole of the North American trumpet creeper, *Campsis radicans.* (Photo by T. S. Elias)

Leaves as Propagules

Some plants have a remarkable facility to propagate from small parts of the plant. This characteristic has been much used by gardeners and agriculturalists for growing new plants from cuttings. In some cases, leaves alone can be used as the unit of propagation. In other plants, the leaves actually produce rows of new plants around their margins.

Perhaps the best-known examples of leaves that produce new plants are found in the succulent genera *Kalanchoë* and *Bryophyllum.* In the case of *Bryophyllum,* the life-plant of Bermuda, when a mature leaf falls from the plant it immediately begins to give rise to a circle of new plants around the margins at the indentation of the teeth. Once the new plants are produced, with minute leaves and roots, the parent leaf dies. While the leaves remain attached to the plant they do not produce any plantlets, but once they are mature they can be detached and will rapidly begin to sprout the new plants. In the case of *Kalanchoë,* the plantlets are produced on the leaves while they are still attached to the parent plant.

Bryophyllum and *Kalanchoë* are both succulent, fleshy leaved plants. This tendency to reproduce from leaves is most common in succulent plants. Several other genera of succulents have species that propagate directly from their leaves, for example *Sedum* and the familiar houseleek, or *Sempervivum,* generate a completely new plant from a single leaf cutting. Other house or garden plants that are easily reproduced from leaves include *Mesembryanthemum* and some species of *Begonia* and of *Peperomia,* a fleshy-leaved member of the black pepper family, Piperaceae. African violet growers have long known that *Saintpaulia* and other members of this family will grow from leaf cuttings. In this case, many of the African violets that propagate from leaves are not succulents.

Propagation from leaves or cuttings is what is known as vegetative reproduction, that is, a new plant has been produced without the sexual process of crossing with another plant to yield a seed. This has the advantage to the horticulturist that the new plant will be a genetically identical clone of its single parent, resembling the parent in all features. This will lead to a more uniform group offspring than the more variable plants resulting from sexual reproduction. This is one reason why horticulturists have made good use of leaf propagation.

Perhaps you have also reproduced a cactus in this way by taking a leaflike piece of a prickly pear and planting it in soil. This is also vegetative reproduction, but it is not from the leaf since in the case of a cactus each segment is part of the stem. The leaves are reduced to spines in the prickly pear and most other cacti. However, these stem cuttings of cactus work in the same way as the leaf cuttings of a *Saintpaulia.*

Since most leaves that are capable of reproduction belong to fleshy desert plants, this must be an adaptation to desert life. When a long drought occurs, most of the plant may die. It would be enough to have a single leaf survive, sheltered by a mass of dead ones above, for the plant to produce a new generation.

BELOW: Closeup of the propagules on the leaf of a cultivated *Kalanchoë.*

OVERLEAF: The leaves of *Kalanchoë daigremontiana* from Madagascar, a succulent plant that produces propagules or bulbils along the margins of the leaves.

LEAVES AS PROPAGULES

Leaf Hairs

The male Mullein or Higtaper hath broad leaves, very soft whitish and downy, in the midst of which riseth up a stalk, straight, single, and the same whitish all over, with a hoary down. . . . The female Mullein hath likewise many white woolly leaves, set upon a hoary cottony upright stalk of the height of foure or five cubits.

The great Mouse-eare hath great and large leaves, thick and full of substance: the stalkes and leaves bee hoary and white, with a silken mossinesse in handling like silke, pleasant and faire in view.

JOHN GERARD,
Herball

Y_{ou} probably know examples of plants that have obviously hairy leaves, such as the mullein *(Verbascum)* with its soft velvety coat or the fuzzy leaves of the famous edelweiss of the Swiss mountains. Many leaves that look glabrous or hairless from a distance turn out to have a dense coat of hairs when examined with a magnifying glass. The different hues that one observes on different leaves are often caused by the way the light catches the hairs on the leaves. The leaves of many plants are in fact quite hairy. Hairs are more common on the lower surfaces of the leaves, leaving the upper surface hairless so that it can gather the light necessary for photosynthesis. However in some cases, particularly in high-altitude plants like the edelweiss, hairs occur on the upper surface to screen the extremely intense light or to conserve warmth.

Many other familiar plants have hairy leaves. The scientific name for the forget-me-not is *Myosotis*, which means "mouse ear." This is because of the soft furriness of the leaf caused by the presence of a hairy covering.

We will see that leaf hairs, like almost any other feature of the leaf, are varied both in their structure and in their function. Technically plant hairs are termed trichomes, from the Greek word *trichoma* for a growth of hair. Trichomes are any outgrowths of the leaf epidermis and also of the shoots and roots.

It is fascinating to look at the lower surface of a leaf under a powerful microscope and to examine the details of the hairs. They may be simple structures made up of a single cell or they may be multicellular, or divided into a number of cells. They can also be almost any shape, from thin, needlelike hairs to fat, barrel-shaped structures. In some cases the trichomes are just small, knoblike protrusions from the leaf surface, in which case the leaf surface is said to be papillate. The majority of plant hairs are unbranched, but in some plant families complicated branched hairs occur. When the separate cells emerge from a central point in a starlike pattern, they are stellate or starlike; when they are branched like a tree, they are dendritic. Hairs can be T-shaped or even in storied tiers, in which case they are termed candelabra type because of their resemblance to candelabras. Disclike hairs on the central stalk are termed peltate and occur in a number of plant families, such as the bromeliads, where they are extremely important, as we shall see.

Plant taxonomists have used the features of hairs in making their classifications. Similar kinds of hair structure often occur in unrelated plant families, showing that the same hair type must have evolved independently many times. However, certain plant groups have stellate hairs and others do not, and the hair type is often quite useful for the definition of individual species. The tropical plant family Malpighiaceae, or the Barbados cherry family, nearly always has a unique type of two-armed, unicellular hairs that are so characteristic of that family that they are termed malpighiaceous hairs. The taxonomists will also describe the quantity of hairs covering a leaf with such terms as puberulous for a light covering, tomentose for a thicker covering, hirsute for a shaggy appearance, or lanate for a woolly look. This is often useful for the definition of species, although caution is needed because hair density can sometimes vary with the habitat of the individual plant.

The variety of hair types and of quantity of hair covering,

termed pubescence, occurs in plants because hairs have various different functions. Many leaves, especially of plants that grow in extreme climates such as deserts or exposed mountain slopes, have a dense covering of hairs, often on both surfaces. Examination shows that these are usually air-filled hairs that form a closely interlocking coating so that they function much like the fur coat of an animal to give protection against extremes of climate. Such a thick coating of hairs helps to protect a leaf from overheating because of strong sun rays or it can help to avoid loss of heat by irradiation. Most important of all, a pubescence can reduce water loss from the plant because the transpiration or evaporation of water through the stomata is reduced. It is not by chance that there are many hairy plants in the desert, in steppe habitats, and on mountain slopes. For example, in the tropics in the Andean highlands the dominant plant of the páramo habitat, which is open grassland, is a member of the aster family, *Espeletia*. The many species of this genus are covered by a dense mass of silky white hair. This protects them from the cold winds that sweep across the páramo.

Some leaves are protected against too much irradiation by their hairy coat. It has been shown that when the felty mass of hair is scraped off the leaves of the coltsfoot *(Tussilago)*, the leaves become much lighter in color because part of the chlorophyll is destroyed by excess light. In 1918 a German scientist, G. Haberlandt, compared the transpiration from a leaf of betony *(Stachys)*, with the silky, hairy covering removed from the upper surface, with that of a normal pubescent leaf. He found that the transpiration doubled when the hairs were removed. It is therefore not surprising that many desert plants are protected by a hairy covering which reduces their water loss in that arid environment. Hairs then can be protection for the plant against heat, cold, and excess sunlight. For this type of protection it is not necessary for the hairs to be specially modified. The requirement for the plant is simply that the hairs be densely distributed in an interlaced pattern. Some types of hairs will obviously function better than others to form such a pattern.

The hairs of many plants are glandular. This type of hair often has an enlarged, roundish tip from which secretions are made. Glandular hairs occur in a surprisingly large number of plants, for example on the leaves and especially the leaf petiole of many species of brambles *(Rubus)*. They are also common in mints and in many members of the aster family. The purpose of glands is to secrete substances. Glandular hairs secrete a variety of substances, each with different functions. Glandular hairs may secrete sticky substances to trap insects, as in some insectivorous plants (see Chapter 11), or they may secrete aromatic compounds to attract pollinating insects, or other compounds to repel predatory insects. Other glandular hairs may be sticky just to protect the plant against predation by small insects. Glandular hairs may also produce mucilage, a slimy substance that is common in many plants, especially around the leaf bases of many monocotyledons, such as the maranta and rapatea families.

Some hairs are hooked at the apex. It is interesting to note that hooked hairs are especially common on the leaves of climbing plants, for example in the hop *(Humulus)* or in some of the clambering species of bedstraw *(Galium)*. The obvious function of these hooked hairs is to facilitate the grasp of the plant as it climbs.

The hairs on some climbing plants increase the roughness of their surface. The leaves or other parts with such rough hairs will slide down the surface on which they are resting less easily because of the hairs.

The leaf hairs of some plants function as water-absorbing organs. This is most important in the bromeliad family, Bromeliaceae. This group has characteristic umbrella-shaped, peltate, scalelike hairs. The majority of bromeliads are epiphytes, or air plants, which perch in the trees or even on telegraph poles and wires in a more urban environment. Epiphytes have difficulty obtaining water. In most epiphytic bromeliads the rosette of tightly overlapping leaves forms a watertight tank which traps rainwater. Since the water is trapped in the leaves it is not available to the roots, which are the normal water-absorption organs of most flowering plants. In the case of bromeliads the scale-hairs have developed the ability to absorb water. Many experiments using radioactive substances and dyes have proven that these leaf hairs are capable of water absorption.

There are many other fascinating aspects to the leaf tanks of the bromeliads. Many organisms live in the precious stores of water up in the forest crown. There are thousands of small, amoebalike, unicellular organisms floating in the water; a species of the insectivorous bladderworts and even tadpoles live there. The tadpoles of one species of frog are transported from the forest floor on the back of the mother and deposited by her in the relative safety of the water tank high in the trees. They develop there and return to the forest floor once they have developed into small frogs.

Umbrellalike hairs cover the entire leaf surface of many bromeliads, not only the area of the water tank at the base. The hairs often have the stomata underneath them shaded by the top part of the hair. This functions to reduce water evaporation by transpiration, a loss reduction which is crucial for the survival of epiphytic plants that have to withstand the long dry periods between rains. Because air plants are not rooted in the soil like most species, they are in a virtual desert in the dry season. Consequently their protective covering of peltate hairs that cover so much of the surface area is one of many modifications to enable them to prosper in what would be an impossible environment for many plants.

The bromeliads are not the only plant group with water-absorbing hairs. For example, the orchids *Eria* and *Pholidota* also form water tanks. In the leaf base they have hairs which have an elongated basal cell, two or three intermediate cells above, and a tuft of one to seven elongated cells that project above the epidermis in small tufts. These function as water-absorbing organs.

Some hairs function in the reverse of the bromeliad type, that is, they secrete water. A water-secreting organ on a plant is called a hydathode, and some hydathodes are formed from hairs. Guttation is the process of secreting drops of water when the hydrostatic pressure in the water-conducting system of a plant has reached a certain pressure. You may have kept a dumbcane *(Dieffenbachia)* as a houseplant and noticed it dripping from the leaf tips. This procedure, which can be a nuisance for your carpet, is guttation. It happens when plants receive more water than they need, and the hydathodes are a sort of safety valve that enables excess water to be removed. In many plants this occurs around the leaf margins at the tips of the veins, but in others it is specially adapted hairs that are the hydathodes. Beans *(Phaseolus)* have hairs which function as hydathodes, as do the stinging hairs of some nettles *(Urtica)*.

One of the most important functions of leaf hairs is that of protection against predators. This is especially important in young leaves. It is often noticeable that the youngest leaves on a plant are more hairy than the older ones. The hairs are formed early in the life of the leaf and fall off or become sparsely spread by the time it is mature. The young leaves of a plant are tender and mechanically soft and it is at that time that they require the most protection from leaf eaters. One such defense is the development of a dense covering of unpleasant hairs. Dense hair cover and glandular hairs that secrete unpleasant chemicals often combine to give the leaf a good chance of surviving to maturity. Various experiments have shown that slugs and snails are reluctant to walk over extremely hairy leaves. The German scientist Otto Renner showed that small garden snails avoided the hairy leaves of wild strawberry *(Fragaria)* or of *Potentilla*. In other plants the hairs have become spinous, which is an effective protection against some browsing animals. Even the minute leaf hairs have been brought into the continuous battle in nature of predator versus prey.

In other chapters of this book we discussed the functioning of some of the most specialized leaf hairs, those that sting (Chapter 10) and those that assist the plant to capture insects (Chapter 11) in the carnivorous plants.

Examine a few leaves closely and look for the variety of hair types and the beauty that the hairs sometimes lend to the general appearance of the plants. Plant organs that do not have hairs are termed glabrous, so be sure that you do not search for hair only on glabrous leaves!

ABOVE: The incredibly long marginal leaf hairs of a cloud-forest plant from Colombia.

BELOW: Many of the plants of the Páramo of Colombia, where it is cold and windy, are extremely hairy. The hairs form a layer of insulation. The *Espeletia* plants scattered over this landscape are a good example of hairy leaves.

ABOVE: The leaf margins of this popular *Begonia, B. mazae viridis*, have conspicuous hairs.

OPPOSITE PAGE: The hairy covering of the leaves of *Stachys olympica* from southern Europe.

The yellow flowers of a hairy *Espeletia* from the Páramo of Colombia growing together with the melastome *Bucquetia glutinosa.*

LEFT: Bromeliads are usually epiphytes or air plants that perch on trees or any other convenient surface, such as these telephone wires in Trinidad. The water tanks with their water-absorbing leaf hairs are essential for the leaves' survival in this arid environment.

BELOW LEFT: A leaf of *Jatropha gossypifolia* from Sri Lanka is pubescent and hairy.

BELOW RIGHT: A dense, wooly pubescence gives this wild vine from Sumatra a white leaf undersurface.

LEAF HAIRS

OPPOSITE PAGE, TOP AND BOTTOM: Many desert plants are extremely hairy. The hairs protect them from excessive water loss from transpiration. Both *Chamaesyce* from the dry Galápagos and this species of *Ptilotus* from Central Australia are examples of hairy desert leaves.

BELOW: This member of the nettle family, *Pilea pubescens,* has conspicuous leaf hairs.

Black-and-white illustrations of leaf hairs and leaf surfaces at high magnifications made with a scanning electron microscope.

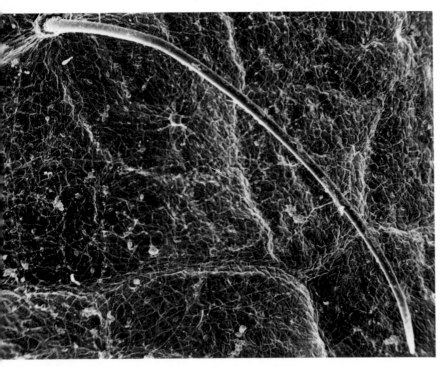

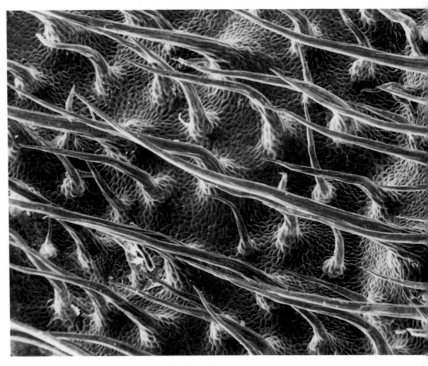

ABOVE: The simple hair type of *Hirtella physophora,* one of the ant-cavity leaves described in Chapter 12 (magnified 164×).

BELOW: The leaf surface of *Piper auritum* near a vein, showing simple hairs and pearl glands (320×).

ABOVE: The leaf hairs of *Tibouchina urvilleana* (164×).

BELOW: The lower leaf surface of *Mascagnia macroptera,* showing flat, appressed hairs and the stomata (165×).

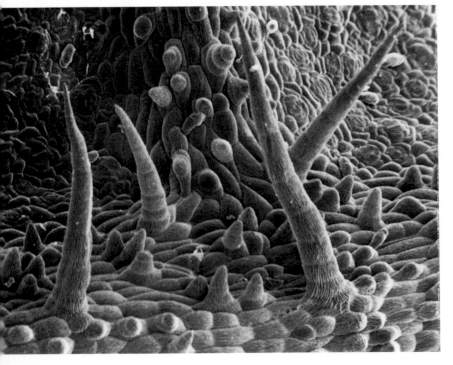

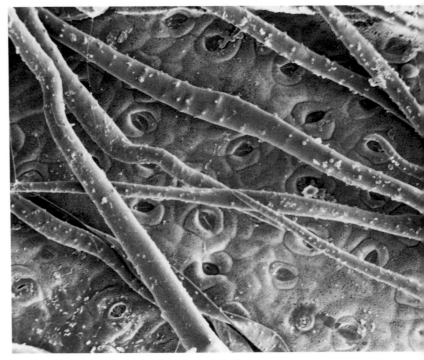

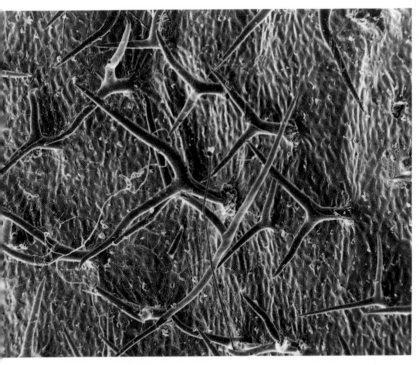

ABOVE: The malpighiaceous hairs of *Peixotoa reticulata,* which are simple, T-shaped, unicellular hairs (165×).

BELOW: The peltate hairs of a species of *Olea* (160×).

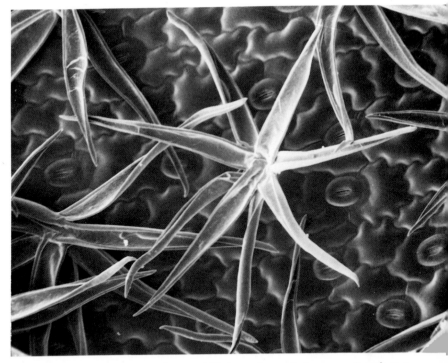

ABOVE: The lower leaf surface of *Platycerium algloense* showing a stellate hair and the stomata (320×).

BELOW: The peltate hairs of *Eleagnus angustifolia* (240×).

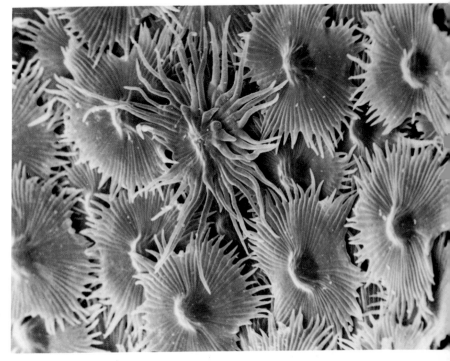

TOP, RIGHT: The lower leaf surface of *Cissus roinieriana,* showing hairs and a large pearl gland (160×).

BOTTOM RIGHT: The stinging hairs of the common nettle *(Urtica dioica),* which resemble hypodermic needles (165×).

BELOW: The glandular hairs of a species of bramble *(Rubus odoratus)* (160×).

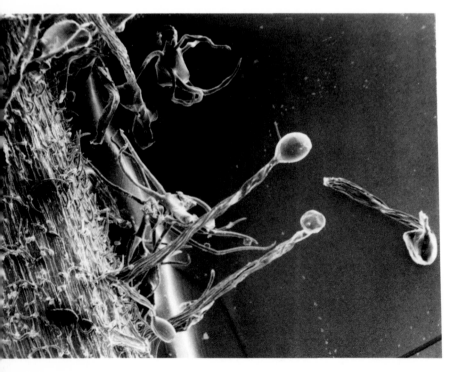

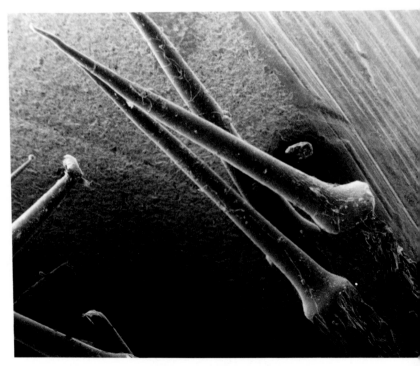

LEAF HAIRS

CHAPTER 15

Epiphylly: Leaves of Burden

The term epiphylly literally means "on leaves", and is derived from the two Greek words *epi* (upon) and *phyllen* (leaf). Therefore flowers that are borne on leaves are epiphyllous, and other plants such as mosses and liverworts that use leaves as their perch are also termed epiphyllous.

We normally associate flowers with separate flowering branches or inflorescences that are well apart from the leaves. Most flowers are borne in inflorescences, but in a few cases nature has economized and the flowers are borne directly on the leaf. This has generally evolved through a gradual fusion of the flowering branches with the leaf stalk and the central nerve of the leaf. There are in fact quite a number of plant species in which this has occurred, for example, in the epiphyllous orchid *Pleurothallis cardiochila* shown in the photograph. The entire genus *Phyllonoma* in the family Grossulariaceae is epiphyllous. This small genus of low trees and shrubs occurs in the mountains of Mexico and Central America. The African genera *Phyllobotryon*, *Phylloclinium*, and *Mocquerysia* in the flacourtia family all have flowers borne on the leaf blade or leaf stalk, and the genus *Tapura* of South America and Africa has inflorescences borne on the petioles in most species and on the leaf blade in two Peruvian Amazon species.

Fern fronds are compound leaves subdivided into many leaflets called pinnae, which can in turn be divided into pinnules. The leaves or fronds of ferns are often covered with little brown dots or streaks on their lower surface. These are the sori, which are the reproductive organs of ferns. Ferns do not bear flowers; instead, they reproduce by an alternation of generations. The fern plants which we know are the sporophyte generation; these produce asexual spores which germinate to produce a small, usually flat plant called the gametophyte. It is the gametophyte which produces asexual organs where true fertilization takes place. After fertilization, the zygote formed develops into a new sporophyte, or a fern plant. The minute, dustlike spores are produced in the sporangia, which are really small spore-bearing sacs. These are usually clustered into groups called sori, which can be seen on the undersurface of many fern leaves.

There is a great variation in the patterns in which the sori are arranged on the leaf. They can be in a straight row, scattered all over the leaf, or in lines. They can be at the center of the frond or around the margin. In a few, more specialized ferns they are borne on special spore-bearing fronds which are quite different from the sterile ones. An overemphasis on the pattern of sori by early taxonomists led to the production of unsatisfactory artificial classifications. The spores are released into the air by a clever mechanism. The sporangium outer layer contains a row of cells, termed the annulus, which comes under great tension by the time the spores are mature. The sporangium wall then breaks and the annulus flips around, casting spores out into the atmosphere. The fern spores are extremely light and are easily blown away by the wind which ensures that the spores get away from the leaves and are widely distributed.

The epiphyllous flowers and the fern spores described above are an integral part of the plant that bears them. There are, however, a large number of smaller plants, mainly in the liverwort and lichen groups, that make their living perched on leaves. These epiphyllous liverworts are not parasites because they do not gain any nutrition from their host. Like the epiphytes, or air plants, the epiphyllous plants merely use their hosts as a perch. They are particularly common in tropical rainforests and in cloud forests. They are obviously an inconvenience to the host plants because they obscure light and impede photosynthesis. This is one of the reasons why many tropical plants, although evergreen, shed their leaves all the time. This casts off the burden of their epiphyllous flora.

Liverworts are primitive plants which together with mosses form the division of plants called bryophytes. The epiphyllous liverworts are usually leafy liverworts, that is, they produce a flattened and prostrate leafy stem. In contrast, many other liverworts consist of a flattened and undifferentiated structure called a thallus. The liverworts were formerly used for liver ailments, hence the name liverwort and their scientific name, Hepaticae, which comes from the Greek word for liver. In the tropics, many of the leafy forms become adapted to the epiphyllous habitat and form a shaggy covering on the leaves of many forest trees.

Lichens are plants which are a strange mixture of an algae and a fungus growing together in a symbiotic relationship. They have grown so much together that the lichens have their own characteristic morphology. The lichen is made up of fungal hyphae, or filaments, with algal cells interspersed. The algal cells absorb water and carry out photosynthesis while the fungi obtain their nutrients from the algal cells. There are many lichens that have adapted the epiphyllous habit, but they occupy many other habitats such as rocks or tree barks. Some are tree epiphytes, like *Usnea barbata*, the old man's beard, which hangs from trees in a similar fashion to Spanish moss.

One of the other phenomena commonly found on leaves is insect galls, which are discussed in more detail in Chapter 19.

BELOW: Ferns reproduce by spores borne in sori on a leaf surface instead of flowers. The characteristic pattern of the sori of *Alsophila sinuata* from Sri Lanka.

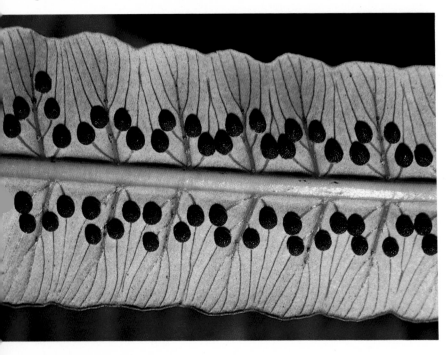

ABOVE: This rainforest leaf from near Manaus, Brazil, is covered with the growth of an epiphyllous liverwort that uses the leaf as a perch. Epiphyllous liverworts are abundant in tropical rainforests.

BELOW: An attractive, star-shaped epiphyllous lichen on a leaf in the forests of Kinabalu, Sabah.

OPPOSITE PAGE: The sori of this *Dipteris* fern are scattered all over the lower surface of the frond without any distinct pattern.

RIGHT: The sori of this fern *(Adiantum trapeziforme)* are borne around the margin of the fronds.

BELOW: The sori of the fern *Blechnum occidentale* occur in two central rows on each frond.

BELOW: The terminal sori of *Davallia solida,* a fern from Queensland, Australia.

LEAVES OF BURDEN

RIGHT: Attractive red galls on the leaf of a silver maple *(Acer saccharinum)* near Washington, D.C.

Raindrops often form attractive patterns on leaves as they dry out after a shower.

ABOVE: On the fern *Dicranopteris* from Kinabalu, Sabah.

RIGHT: On *Cissampelos pareira* from Sri Lanka.

CHAPTER 16

Modified Leaves

Plants become climbers, in order . . . to reach the light, and to expose a large surface of their leaves to its action. This is effected by climbers with wonderfully little expenditure of organized matter in comparison with trees, which have to support a load of heavy branches by a massive trunk.

Tendrils consist of various organs in a modified state, namely, leaves, flower-peduncles, branches and perhaps stipules.

CHARLES DARWIN,
*The Movements and Habits
of Climbing Plants*

We think of leaves as the flat, green organs of plants. However, there are many ways in which leaves become modified into other structures to perform different functions for plants. For example, tendrils of climbing plants and thorns of spinous plants are often modified leaves. The bulb of an onion is a cluster of specialized leaves, and the scales that protect the winter buds of so many of our trees are also specially adapted leaves, as are the plant structures known as bracts and stipules. All of them have specialized functions to perform.

If you examine the flower branches of most plants you will find at the base of the flowerstalk or on the stalk itself small, green, scalelike structures which are called *bracts*. These are really modified leaves and they often function in the young buds as a protection around the tiny developing flower. In many plants the bracts are so small that they now have little or no function and often drop off before the flower is fully open. They are really evidence that the flower parts are all modified leaves that have evolved from primitive plant forms into a unit with a very special function, that of reproduction.

However, in some often familiar species of plants the bracts have developed a new function and have become more like petals. These brightly colored bracts are for the purpose of attracting pollinating insects or other animals. The attractive red parts of the poinsettia, which make it so familiar as a winter holiday decoration, are not petals but bracts, which is why they are leaf-shaped. The flower of a poinsettia is only the small yellow core at the center, which is not bright enough to draw the attention of any pollinator.

Plants with conspicuous bracts, such as the poinsettia, tend to be well known because they have also attracted the attention of the horticulturist, who has made use of the color for display purposes and has developed many different variations, as we can see from the variety of white to pink to deep-red poinsettias available in the stores around Christmastime. Other familiar plants with colorful bracts are the dogwoods and the *Bougainvillea,* one of the most used tropical ornamentals. The dogwood inflorescence is a cluster of numerous drab, yellow-green flowers that are grouped together to form a central circle or eye that contrasts with the four to six large white to pink bracts which circle the flower cluster. The bee pollinators of the dogwood are attracted by the conspicuous white bracts.

A Nanticoke Indian legend tells of a chief who had four beautiful daughters. Their father promised that he would give them to the suitors who brought the best gifts. His home was soon filled with many furs and other gifts. The gods were angry at such behavior from a chief so they turned him into a tree. The tree was a small, bent tree that would be dwarfed by the oaks and maples. The four white bracts are said to be the four daughters of the chief, and the flowers in the middle the gifts brought by the would-be husbands.

The Indian paintbrush *(Castilleja),* a familiar plant to the residents of the western United States, is also attractive because of its bright orange and red "brushes," which are really bracts, not petals.

Many of the bromeliads, relatives of the pineapple, that decorate the trees in the tropical forests of the New World have brightly colored bracts. Behind these red or orange bracts are the cylindrical flowers that have nectar inside the tubular petals. Humming-birds are attracted by the showy bracts and so their search for the nectar is made easy. Red is the color that attracts birds best of all, and many of the tropical plants with bright red or orange bracts are visited by nectar-gathering hummingbirds which incidentally carry pollen from one plant to another. The bird-of-paradise flower *(Strelitzia)* is a bird-pollinated flower that also is made attractive by its colorful bracts. That plant has many relations in the tropics in the genus *Heliconia*. The Heliconias have been used as ornamentals by the Brazilian artist and landscape designer Roberto Burle-Marx, who has made extensive use of the great variety of colors found in the bracts of the wild species.

The national flower of the Caribbean country of Trinidad is one of the most beautiful examples of showy bracts. The chaconia *(Warszewiczia coccinea)* is a member of the coffee family. It is a shrub or small tree whose bracts are as showy as those of a poinsettia.

The ultimate in bracts is the large sheathing one called a spathe which envelops the inflorescence of certain families of monocotyledons, especially in the arum lily family, where it is usually persistent through flowering, and the palms, where it is often deciduous. The Panama hat family, Cyclanthaceae, is another family with the flowers in a spadix, or spiky inflorescence, enclosed by a spathe, but the spathe is usually deciduous in that family. The spathe is often green and inconspicuous, while in the palms it is usually hard and woody. In fact, the spathe of one of the Amazonian palms is so large that it is used as a temporary canoe by the Indian natives to cross a river. The showiest spathes occur in various members of the arum lily family, especially in the genus *Anthurium*. Many species of *Anthurium* are cultivated as houseplants because of their bright red or scarlet spathes. They are often waxy and look like plastic. Many other aroids have brightly colored spathes which often surround most of the spike and can trap pollinating beetles inside. The other plant family with a spathe and spadix is the tropical Asian group the screw pines, or Pandanaceae, which are now cultivated around the tropics and subtropics.

We have seen how the modified leaves that we call bracts have taken on the function normally performed by petals, that of pollinator attraction. In addition to birds, various plants with bright bracts attract butterflies, another group of animals to which red and orange colors are appealing. Next time you see a dogwood, poinsettia, or a bougainvillea, examine the flowers carefully and observe the small, inconspicuous flowers that are surrounded by the colorful bracts.

At the base of the petiole of many leaves you can find two small, leaflike structures called *stipules*. Generally, like bracts, stipules are tiny and have little function, and often fall off early in the development of the leaf. They are parts of the leaf and vary from small green blades which carry on photosynthesis to thin, transparent, scalelike structures. However, there are many examples in the plant kingdom where stipules have become modified to other functions. The Japanese quince, the woodruff (Asperula), and the garden pea are good examples of plants with large, leaf-like, photosynthesizing stipules. In other plants stipules have become modified into tendrils (see below), ant houses (see Chapter 12), or spines.

The stipules of many plants have become spines which protect the plant (see Chapter 10). The legume or bean family is one where stipules usually occur, and in several, such as the black locust (Robinia pseudoacacia), the stipules have become spines. In this tree, which is widely cultivated outside its native range in the Appalachian and Ozark mountains, there are a pair of sharp spines at the junction of the compound leaf with the stem. Similar structures occur in the desert ironwood (Olneya tesota) of the western United States and especially in the acacias. In the case of the acacias, some species have spines that are inhabited by ants; they are described in detail in Chapter 12. The spines of the acacias and other legumes are stipules which have been modified for the function of protection of their plant from predation by browsing mammals and other large leaf eaters.

In many plants the stipules are scalelike structures which protect the leaf buds. The bud scales of the beech, oak, magnolia, and many members of the fig family are stipules. As the bud unfolds, these large stipules drop off since they have performed their protective function. In the tulip tree (Liriodendron tulipifera), they envelop the young leaves for some time but fall off soon after the leaves reach full size. In the European yellow vetchling (Lathyrus aphaca), the stipules are large and leaflike and perform the normal function of leaves while the leaflets of this member of the pea family have become modified into tendrils.

Nature has found many ways to make good use of these normally small appendages of leaves through adaptations.

Tendrils are yet another form of leaf modification which occurs on climbing plants. Vines need tendrils to grasp onto shrubs and trees to lift the plant upward toward the sunlight. In gardening we make use of this fact to train climbing plants such as peas or beans over trellises or up walls. Tendrils are either modified leaves, stems, or stipules, depending on the particular plant. They are leaves or stipules without blades that have become threadlike. The sweet pea, grapevine, Virginia creeper, morning glory, and clematis are all familiar garden plants with tendrils.

Tendrils are interesting because they respond to contact or touch, a phenomenon that is termed thigmotropism. When a tendril extends from the plant and comes into contact with an object such as a pole or a branch, it immediately begins to coil around it. This is effected through differential growth, where the cells away from the side of the point of contact elongate quickly and more rapidly than those on the side touching the object. This causes them to twine around. The tendrils of different species may coil clockwise or counterclockwise. In the sweet pea and other plants, the tendril coils around a pole and then contracts spirally, thus drawing the whole vine upward and closer for support. In a few plants such as the Virginia creeper (Parthenocissus quinquefolia) and Boston ivy (P. tricuspidata), the tendrils have dish-shaped cups which adhere to wood as well as to brick and stone. After the cup is firmly attached, the tendrils of the plants also contract and then draw the plants upward.

Climbing plants have long been a subject of curiosity to naturalists. The English naturalist Charles Darwin wrote a book entitled The Movements and Habits of Climbing Plants, which has never been surpassed. He devoted over one hundred pages to tendril-bearing plants and went into fascinating details about their climbing behavior. For example, he observed that, in the plants he studied, the rate of revolution of tendrils varied from one to five hours. He found that the tendrils of one of the passion flower vines, Passiflora gracilis, were the most sensitive. A bit of platinum wire of 1.23 milligrams placed on a tendril caused it to become hooked. The tendril of this Passiflora began to move distinctly only twenty-five seconds after a touch. Many early naturalists were fascinated by tendrils; the founder of North American botany, Asa Gray, observed that the tendrils of Sicyos in the cucumber family began to move just thirty seconds after a touch.

Darwin also described leaf-climbers. These are climbing plants without tendrils that climb with the aid of normal leaves. In these plants the petioles are clasping and sensitive and wrap around an object of contact. This occurs in some species of Clematis and Tropaeolum or the much cultivated garden nasturtium.

The rattan palm (Calamus) of tropical Asia is a most important source of fiber used for basketwork, chairs, and cord. This group of palms is unusual because they are climbers and the leaves have become adapted to this habit, which is rare in palms. The upper leaflets of the fronds are barbed "grappling hooks" that catch onto the bark and stems of trees. With these hooks to secure them, the rattans can easily climb.

Whether a tendril is formed from a leaf or a stipule, it is still an effective way of ascent for plants that have chosen the climbing habit rather than the support of a thick, woody trunk.

Nature protects the most valuable parts of its organisms well. The buds containing the embryonic leaves are obviously vital and those leaf buds are usually protected by a series of bud scales, which are also modified leaves. These are best developed in the trees of the temperate region because by the time they shed their leaves the next year's buds have formed, ready to burst open as soon as spring arrives. These winter buds of many trees are protected by tough, waterproof, overlapping scales. Each tree has characteristic bud formation and most species can be identified from a twig with buds. The buds protect the embryonic leaves from frost damage, drying out, and also insect and fungal attack. The latter function explains why the buds of many trees are sticky, as in the case of the horse chestnut.

In spring the buds burst open and the scales, having performed their function, are shed. However, they leave a ring of scars where they were attached. The characteristic pattern of these bud scars is a useful feature for the identification of trees. Each year a circular row of bud scales remains so that one can determine the age of twigs by counting the number of groups of annual bud-scale scars, which remain conspicuous on the twigs for five or more years.

The function of *bulbs* is also to carry plants through the winter. A bulb is formed by a series of concentric layers of modified leaves that are tightly packed together on top of one another just above the roots and usually below the surface of the soil. Perhaps the most familiar bulb in our daily life is the onion. The onion plant has tubular green leaves above the ground, but below the ground a bulb is formed from the white leaf bases. The bulbs of the onion and the hyacinth are formed of many layers of scales enclosed in a membraneous tunic, but bulbs may be naked scales as in many of the lilies. The bulb scales enclose the bud with the embryonic above-ground leaves and flower stalks.

In bulbous plants the aerial parts die down each winter and only the swollen underground bulb remains, protecting the embryo like a bud on a tree branch. The bulb's other main function is to store nutrients for the plant so that it can quickly shoot up in the spring. Bulbs store carbohydrates in the form of sugars and, less commonly, starches, which is why some bulbs, such as the onion, are important foods. Bulbs produce small bulbs in the axils of the scales. These are called bulbils and are the way of reproducing many bulbous plants through the separation of the bulbils from the parent plant. Many of our commonly cultivated spring flowers, such as the daffodil, hyacinth, narcissus, and tulip, produce bulbs.

True bulbs are always structures formed from modified leaves. Many other underground overwintering structures of plants are mistakenly called bulbs, such as the corm of a crocus or gladiolus or the tuber of a dahlia. These are modified roots, not leaves, although they serve the same function of underground food storage and reproduction.

The leaf is an adaptable organ. Under various pressures of natural selection, in response to the environmental needs of the plants, leaves have become adapted to diverse functions that enable their particular species to survive. Whether it is a defense against predators, as in the acacia spines, or food storage through the winter, as in a daffodil bulb, each leaf modification has a purpose in nature.

RIGHT: Stipules are usually appendages at the base of leaves, as in this *Cespedesia* from Chocó, Colombia.

MODIFIED LEAVES

ABOVE: The stipules of many members of the fig family (Moraceae) are large and protect the young leaves, as in this rubber plant *(Ficus elastica)* from India.

OPPOSITE PAGE, LEFT: The spines of acacias are modified stipules. This one is *Acacia rorudiana* from the Galápagos.

OPPOSITE PAGE, RIGHT: The extraordinary modified leaflet apices of *Calliandra haematocephala* from Brazil.

ABOVE: Tendrils of a vine from Amazonian Brazil.

LEFT: The tendrils of a young leaf of a passion flower vine from Manaus, Brazil.

MODIFIED LEAVES

ABOVE AND OPPOSITE PAGE: These *Opuntia echios* cacti from the Galápagos have no leaves. The stem has taken over the function of the leaves and the leaves are reduced to spines.

MODIFIED LEAVES

RIGHT: The red color of the Poinsettia *(Euphorbia pulcherrima)* comes from the modified flower leaves, or bracts, which give it the beauty that has made it a holiday favorite. In Jamaica, it becomes a large shrub.

BELOW: Bracts of a Poinsettia in Jamaica.

OVERLEAF: Bracts of *Mussaenda erythrophylla*, a West African member of the coffee family.

ABOVE: The showy bracts of *Warszewiczia coccinea*, a showy Amazonian member of the coffee family that is the national flower of Trinidad.

RIGHT: Many bromeliads have showy bracts, as in this *Aechmea chantinii* from Amazonian Brazil.

BELOW: The tropical *Bougainvillea* also gets its beauty from the colorful bracts.

TOP RIGHT: The colorful bracts of this Amazonian *Psychotria* in the coffee family surround the small, inconspicuous flowers and attract birds to them.

BOTTOM RIGHT: The leaf that encloses the flower head of the aroids is called a spathe, and can be very showy, as in this *Anthurium scherzerianum* from Costa Rica.

BELOW: An *Anthurium andraeanum* from Colombia with a bright-red, waxy spathe.

154

BELOW: The leaf bracts at the base of the flower heads of an Amazonian sedge.

ABOVE: A modified stem that resembles leaves in a *Hakea nitida* from near Perth, Australia.

OPPOSITE PAGE: A ring of bracts around the base of a flower, called an involucre, occurs in many members of the aster family as well as in the teasels. The teasel *(Dipsacus sylvestris)* is from the eastern coast of North America.

MODIFIED LEAVES

Leaves in Mass

The last red leaf is whirled away,
The roots are blown about the skies

ALFRED, LORD TENNYSON,
"In Memoriam"

November's sky is chill and drear,
November's leaf is red and sear.

SIR WALTER SCOTT,
"Marmion"

A sudden splendor from behind
Flushed all the leaves with rich golden-green.

ALFRED, LORD TENNYSON

And the leaves that are green turn to brown,
And they wither in the wind,
And they crumble in your hand.

PAUL SIMON

We have said much about indi-
vidual leaves, their function, structure, adaptation, and uses.
However, one of the most impressive features of leaves is the
quantity in which they occur. We cannot walk into a park or forest

without seeing the mass of leaves around us. The individual shapes and sizes of the leaves add to the effect of the appearance of a tree. Much of the variety in the form and shape of trees is due to branching patterns and leaf type. It is this assortment of leaf masses that makes our rural landscapes so attractive. In cities, trees are planted for the effects that leafy crowns will create in an urban landscape. In warm climates, trees with leaf crowns are planted to cast shade to create cooler areas for both people and livestock. Trees are pruned into many different shapes to add to their beauty or to create special effects.

An example of such pruning is topiary, where trees or shrubs are cut into elaborate shapes such as animals, urns, or nymphs or are planted to form mazes. This art was popular in old-fashioned gardens and is in vogue again today. The most commonly used trees in topiary are box, privet, arborvitae, and yew.

Another method of training trees is to bring them flat against a wall on a trellis. This technique, called espalier work, is commonly done with apple or pear trees, which can be trained into elaborate, fanlike patterns.

The crowns of trees can consist of a few large leaves at the top of an unbranched stem, as in most palms, tree ferns, and other predominantly tropical plants, or they may be many-branched to cover a wide area. The crown of the saman tree in the photograph shades an area of slightly more than one acre! This is a low-spreading crown. Others can be round or conical as in many of the conifers, such as the spruce that is commonly used as a Christmas tree.

Leaves when they come together in a mass become even more wonderful and amazing than alone. Apart from their basic function, to support life on our planet, they add beauty and enjoyment to our daily life.

The most spectacular example of leaves in mass is seen in the beautiful fall coloring of the trees of the northeastern United States. This region has a much more attractive fall coloring than Europe, not primarily because of the different species of trees, but because of the ideal climate to stimulate the changes. Maples transplanted to Europe never attain the same fall beauty that they have in their native North America. The combination of crisp cold nights and clear sunny days is necessary for vivid coloration to occur. The mild weather of the European fall combined with much cloud cover turns the trees only to brown and dull yellow.

The variety of different tree species also helps to add to the spectacular nature of fall. Each species contributes its own particular color to the patchwork of golds, oranges, yellows, and reds, as the sumac turns scarlet, the red maple a variety of red and orange, the elm yellow, the birch a bright gold, and the basswood bronze.

We all know that something triggers the leaves of temperate trees to change color and eventually drop off. The chemical changes which start this reaction are initiated by changes in day length. Many of the timed happenings in the life of plants, such as flowering, opening of leaf buds, and shedding of leaves, are controlled by this phenomenon called photoperiodism. For example, the poinsettia will not flower unless subjected for a few weeks to the exact day length that stimulates flowering. The shorter daylight in the fall triggers the leaf fall which is technically termed abscission.

Trees must shed their leaves to survive the frosty winter. Well before the leaves are ready to fall off, abscission begins when a zone in the petiole called the abscission zone becomes active and corky material below the zone begins to seal off the scar. The active summer leaves contain many valuable minerals and nutrients, and before the leaf is cut off from supplies these substances are substantially transported out of the leaves to avoid their loss. When this transport of materials begins, the leaves stop producing chlorophyll and other compounds and photosynthesis ceases. The chlorophyll gradually bleaches away and other pigments that have been in the leaf all along begin to show through. These are the yellow xanthophyll and the orange and red carotene. As these pigments start to become visible, the fall mosaic of colors begins to appear. The mixture of carotene and xanthophyll alone produces a wide variety of colors in the range of yellow, orange, and red. These pigments also occur in many familiar foods and give them their attractive color, for example in ears of corn, carrots, and egg yolks.

The richness of fall coloration is enhanced by further chemical reactions which produce pigments called anthocyanins which are scarlet, purple, or blue. The addition of these colors to those of xanthophyll and carotene leads to a blend that yields the full spectrum of fall colors. The trees, however, have lost few nutrients because they have been removed to the trunk and roots. The anthocyanins are manufactured from sugars that remain in the leaf after the nutrient supply is cut off by the formation of the corky abscission zone. The brightest and most vivid fall coloration occurs in years when there is strong fall sunlight because the conversion of sugars to anthocyanins varies from year to year, depending upon the amount of sunlight. The process of abscission is governed by a group of plant hormones that are genetically programmed to function. The mechanism is complex and is only just being worked out in detail by plant physiologists.

The abscission zone consists of a layer of cells whose walls are composed mainly of cellulose and are digested by enzymes in response to hormonal messages. These cells become weakened by the work of the enzymes and the weight of the leaf causes it to fall from the plant. The scar is sealed over by cork or secretions. The process is so complex that recently a whole book of nearly four hundred pages by University of California scientist Dr. Frederick T. Addicott was devoted to abscission.

One strange biological fact about fall coloration is that it has no function for the trees. There is no selective advantage in producing these colors. It is rare to find in nature such things happening for no purpose at all. Coloration occurs after the leaves are no longer of use to the tree. The fallen leaves themselves are of use to the plant since the nutrients that remain in them enter the soil and are recycled. This process of recycling is especially critical in the tropical rainforests where the soil is poor. When the leaves fall from the trees in tropical forests they are recycled with extreme rapidity with the help of fungi. Some mycorrhizal fungi which rot leaves are attached directly to both the leaves and the roots of trees. They thus recycle many of the nutrients directly back into the trees.

In contrast to the broad-leaved deciduous trees, the northern forests also contain many evergreen conifers. These cone-bearing trees belong to an ancient group of plants called gymnosperms. Most conifers are evergreen and have needlelike leaves. It is this mass of small narrow leaves that gives them their characteristic appearance.

The leaf of the conifer is completely different from the broad leaf of most deciduous trees because it is adapted to the evergreen lifestyle. Evergreens must withstand the hardships of winter with its frosts, ice, storms, and snowfall. These leaves are a wonderful design for such extremes of climate. The broad leaves of a maple or oak would be torn to shreds by winter storms or would be weighed down and broken off by the weight of ice. The conifer leaf is narrow and does not catch the wind. It is mechanically strong and is covered by a thick, waxy cuticle that adds to its protection. There are fewer stomata per unit area in the conifers. The needles are arranged in many different ways which give each species its characteristic appearance.

While conifers such as the pines, firs, and the yew have needlelike leaves, others have scalelike leaves instead. In this case the small leaves usually overlap tightly. The giant sequoias and redwoods are good examples of conifers with scalelike leaves. These truly giant trees of the west coast of North America are some of the most majestic trees in the world. Although the trees are giant and have many branches, the individual leaves are tiny scales which measure less than a quarter of an inch in length. The junipers and the cypress trees are also conifers with small, scalelike leaves.

The leaves of many conifers contain resin ducts which are filled with pleasantly scented resin. This acts as a chemical defense against insect attack, particularly important in an evergreen leaf which functions for a much longer time than its deciduous counterpart and consequently cannot afford to be damaged by predators.

Only a few conifers are deciduous, for example, the bald cypress, the ginkgo or Chinese maidenhair tree, and the larches. These all lose their leaves in the fall.

We tend to think of fall leaves as a nuisance because of the constant work they cause as we rake them up. However, these old leaves that the tree has discarded can be put to work as a mulch or compost. Oak leaves, which decompose rather slowly, make a good mulch around large plants such as azaleas. The majority of fall leaves that are softer, such as maple leaves, can be used to make good compost. The leaves are not very rich in nutrients because the trees withdraw the most important substances before they shed their leaves. However, the leaf compost is excellent for conditioning the soil.

We might as well make use of the fantastic production of leaves that nature supplies us with. Arborist Edward Connell of Stamford, Connecticut, has calculated that an average apple tree produces 50,000 to 100,000 leaves and that a fifty-foot sugar maple has 162,500 leaves! This is little in comparison to the 700,000 leaves of an oak tree or the 5 million leaves the almost extinct American elm can produce at maturity. A lot of raking for the owner!

BELOW: The delicate leaf structure of a tree fern in the mountain forests of Cibodja, Java.

ABOVE: The saman tree *(Samanea saman)* has a characteristic flat crown. This tree, on the campus of the University of the West Indies in Trinidad, shades an area of half an acre.

BELOW: Tree ferns, the giants of the ferns, are characteristic of tropical mountain areas. This one is at an elevation of 4,000 feet in the mountains of New Caledonia.

RIGHT: The silhouette of mountain rainforest trees at Ratnapura, Sri Lanka.

BELOW: The massive leaves of the nest fern *(Asplenium nidus)* on a tree trunk in the mountains of Java.

LEAVES IN MASS

BELOW: Palm fronds are grouped together at the apex of a single-branched trunk. This *Corypha umbraculifera* palm flowers after fifty years of growth and then dies. Photographed at Peradeniya, Sri Lanka.

LEAVES IN MASS

166

OPPOSITE PAGE, TOP LEFT: The crown and fruit of a *Ptychosperma* palm from New Guinea.

OPPOSITE PAGE, TOP RIGHT: Topiary is the art of growing and pruning plants into strange shapes. This elephant is in the Singapore Botanical Garden.

TOP LEFT: A South American tree of the Acanthaceae family with spectacular leaves.

BOTTOM LEFT: The needlelike leaves of a Central American pine from Belize.

BELOW: The Greek myrtle, *Myrtus communis.*

OPPOSITE PAGE, BOTTOM LEFT: A topiary lion made with *Helixine soleirolii* and the Kenilworth ivy *(Cymbalaria muralis).*

OPPOSITE PAGE, BOTTOM RIGHT: A mass of leaves of a climbing *Philodendron* on a tree at Lae, New Guinea.

OPPOSITE PAGE, TOP: Fall scene.

OPPOSITE PAGE, BOTTOM: Fall in Vermont.

RIGHT: A fall oak leaf.

BELOW: The varied spectrum of fall colors.

OPPOSITE PAGE: Fall scene.

RIGHT: A spectacular fall maple.

BELOW: Enjoying fall leaves.

Fall in Vermont.

LEAVES IN MASS

Leaves That Move

Here is a hill of brimstone and much more to be admired, here is also the virgin plant, which they terme the sensible tree, which after the least touch of ones hand I see fall down withered, and then againe revived after a little space.

FATHER WHITE,
Briefe Relation (1634), on arrival in Barbados

Right as an aspes leef she gan to quake.

GEOFFREY CHAUCER,
Troilus and Criseyde

We tend to think of leaves as stationary objects because they are attached to plants that are stationary in contrast to the mobile animal kingdom. However, although leafy plants are fixed to the ground by their roots, there are numerous types of movement known in their leaves, such as that of the sensitive Mimosa *(Mimosa pudica)*, which closes when its leaves are touched, and the Venus' flytrap, which, as we have seen earlier, closes its leaves to trap insects.

The great naturalist Charles Darwin was fascinated with plant movements. In fact, he was so attracted by plant movements that he wrote a 500-page book on them that is still one of the best descriptions of this phenomenon *(Power of Movement in Plants).*

Perhaps you have seen a field of sunflowers with all the spectacular yellow-and-black flowers facing in the same direction. This familiar example of movement is actually caused by leaf movement, since the leaves of the plants turn toward the sun and twist the stem and consequently the flowers. You can watch the plant gradually turning as the sun moves across the sky. By morning they have reverted to their former position, ready to follow the sun the next day.

Another plant with leaves that move with the sun is the mallow-weed. The leaves follow the sun across the sky. It is interesting to observe that when a tree trunk shades these leaves, they stop moving. However, they hurriedly change position when the sunlight returns. They too reverse the movement during the night, ready for the path of the sun the next day.

Other leaves turn away from the sun to avoid too much sunlight. This is a common adaptation of desert plants whose leaves often turn vertically away from the sun so that the light strikes the plant at a sharp angle and thus reduces water loss. This is common in some species of the Australian gum trees or *Eucalyptus.*

The Ceará rubber tree of northeastern Brazil *(Manihot glaziovii),* a relative of the cassava plant, has leaves that move. The leaves are digitately compound, like those of a horse chestnut. In the early morning they spread wide open to catch the sun. As the sunlight becomes strong the leaves begin to droop until they are folded against the petiole like an umbrella. This is an adaptation to the arid climate of northeastern Brazil, where the plants of the region must reduce water loss to a minimum. The ability to move its leaves gives the Ceará rubber tree the opportunity both to catch sunlight for photosynthesis in the cool of the early morning and to conserve water by folding the leaves during the midday sun.

In the case of *Mimosa,* the sensitive plant, when the leaflets are touched they immediately fold tightly against one another. If you are patient you can wait and observe them gradually open again. If they are touched again a second time, they remain closed for a longer period. Many children in tropical countries, where *Mimosa* is common, entertain themselves tormenting the plant in this way.

This movement is controlled by remarkably nervelike electrical impulses. Brushing the leaves triggers a fast-moving negative electrical impulse which sets off the leaf movement. Scientists Christine Jones and John Wilson of the University College of North Wales have shown that the leaves of sensitive plants such as *Mimosa* and *Biophytum* also close up when subjected to negative electric shocks. They even close when an antistatic pistol or perspex rod is held half an inch above the leaf without touching it! The leaves close by turgor movement when the cells at the base of the leaflets lose water and grow limp, causing the leaflets to droop. In time they regain their water level and stiffen.

Why would leaves function in this manner? The leaf movements of *Mimosa* and other sensitive plants are most likely to defend the plants against attacking insects. The herbivorous insect landing on such a leaf is immediately frightened or even thrown off the plant by the sudden movements.

Many other plants show "sleep" movements at nightfall. When the plant closes down its photosynthesis factory for the night, the leaves may droop or close up. This can be seen in such familiar plants as beans, jewelweed, *Laburnum,* and *Oxalis,* a common garden weed.

The walking leaf *(Camptosorus rhizophyllus)* is a fern of the Aspleniaceae family that grows on moss-covered rocks. The base of the leaf is at least an inch wide, but it gradually tapers toward the apex, which is drawn out into a narrow, threadlike strand. As this grows it arches over until the tip touches the rock. This takes root and a new plant is formed. Thus each new generation of this plant moves away through this continuous arching over the leaf tip.

The plant which has the most mysterious leaf movements of all is the Asian semaphore or telegraph plant *(Desmodium gyrans),* whose leaves are in an irregular motion all day long. In this plant of the legume family, sometimes all the leaves move in circles and sometimes leaves on one side of the plant stem move up while those on the other side move down. At times it appears to run wild, with some leaves moving upward, others downward, and yet others moving in circles. It has a jerky movement and occasionally stops as if for a short rest. This has been called the most curious leaf movement in the world, and scientists are at a loss to explain the reason for these peculiar girations of the aptly named telegraph plant.

Houseplants grown in a rather dark or unevenly lit room will bend toward the light. They need to be rotated so that they are not completely bent toward the window of the room. This movement is called phototropism, or the positive response of the shoot of a plant toward light. Roots, on the other hand, are negatively phototropic and grow away from light.

Another familiar leaf movement is caused by water shortage or extreme cold, which causes water shortage. This can be seen in Rhododendron leaves on a cold winter's day, when they curl up like cigars and warn people inside their heated houses that it is extremely cold outside.

No description of leaf movements would be complete without an allusion to the compass plant *(Silphium laciniatum)* of the daisy family. The much-divided leaves of this plant *do not move,* but instead they align themselves with the path of the sun, half of them pointing toward the east and the other half toward the west. Thus on a cloudy, sunless day the early explorers of the prairie regions of the west had a compass provided for them by nature from the leaves of the plant!

BELOW: The sensitive leaves and leaflets of a *Mimosa.*

LEFT: This member of the mimosa group of legumes *(Neptunia oleracea)* is a floating aquatic with sensitive leaves similar to the common sensitive plants.

BELOW: The delicate leaves of the sensitive plant, *Mimosa pudica,* which has attractive, fluffy, ball-like flowers.

CHAPTER 19

Patterns of Leaf Damage: The Visiting Cards of Insects

The caterpillar on the leaf
Repeats to thee thy mother's grief.
Kill not the moth or butterfly,
For the Last Judgement draweth nigh.

WILLIAM BLAKE,
"Auguries of Innocence"

Leaf damage might seem an unlikely subject for consideration here, but it is in fact a most interesting subject, which adds a lot of visually attractive patterns to nature around us.

Some animals, such as deer, cows, and goats, eat whole leaves and leave behind nothing but the mowed-down leaf stalk or leaf base. It is the others, mainly insects, that eat only part of the leaf and leave behind telltale and characteristic tracks that are of interest here. Different insects have different methods of leaf eating. Some, such as caterpillars like the gypsy moth larva, start at the leaf margin and eat most or all of the leaf and thus leave little trace of their activity, except a path of destruction and a mess of frass, or droppings. Others eat only part of the leaf and so deposit the story of their life engraved on the leaf as a series of holes or tracks in well-defined patterns.

Insects may perforate the leaves, making holes right through the leaf blade, or they may eat out only part of the leaf tissue, making cavities into the leaves from a single side. Other insects skeletonize the leaves, that is, they eat out all the soft tissue and leave behind only the network of the leaf veins. Some of the leaf skeletons we find in the forest have been formed in this way; others have been formed by the differential action of leaf-rotting fungi. Yet other insects, known as miners, eat out the central contents of the leaf, leaving both the upper and lower epidermis intact. They burrow inside the leaf and mine out the contents on which they feed. The last type of insect that we will consider here is that which causes abnormal growth of the leaf tissue to form their own characteristic homes, called galls, around the larvae.

One of the most interesting features of many leaf-perforating insects, and of almost all miners, is that each species of insect leaves behind a characteristic pattern. Therefore, it is often possible to identify what sort of insect has attacked the leaves merely by the pattern in which it has eaten the leaf. Each insect species leaves behind its "visiting card" carved out of or engraved into the leaf surface.

Insects usually go through several different phases of their life cycle, developing from the egg to the adult stage via the larva and the pupa. It is the larval stage which hatches out of the egg that is the leaf-eating phase. The familiar caterpillars in our gardens are the larvae of butterflies and moths. However, as we shall see, the larvae of other groups of insects are also involved in causing leaf patterns.

Leaf *perforators* may make holes in a scattered, random nature over a leaf surface, or they may produce a pattern. Patterns are produced when they attack only certain parts of a leaf, such as the area next to the junction of the main veins with the center vein. The most distinct perforation patterns are produced when an insect eats through several folds of a leaf while it is in bud. A folded or rolled leaf will have a series of overlapping layers at the same level. If an insect perforates through each layer it will produce an orderly row of identical holes at exactly the same level of the leaf. In the tropics this type of perforation is quite common when certain beetle larvae attack the rolled leaves of various species of *Heliconia* (a relative of the banana), or of species of the *Maranta* or arrowroot family. This is shown in the photograph of a *Heliconia*.

The common houseplant *Monstera*, which is a native of the South American rainforests, would at first sight appear to have been perforated by some strange insect. In fact, the holes in this leaf are natural and are the normal growth pattern of the plant and of its cousin in the same family, *Caladium*. It is this feature which makes them an interesting curiosity as a houseplant. It is not necessary to rear some strange South American insect in your house in order to get the attractive perforated effect of the leaves of *Monstera* and *Caladium*.

Leaf *miners* create feeding passages inside the leaf. The study of these insects is known as hyponomology, from the Greek word *hyponome*, meaning an underground passage. Leaf miners are not a single group of insects in the classification system. They belong to several different orders of insects, showing that the habit of leaf mining has evolved several times in the insects as a way for their larvae to gain access to an excellent and well-protected food source under the leaf epidermis. The most common and important leaf miners are the larvae of moths, or *Lepidoptera*, and of the flies and midges, or *Diptera*. However, leaf-mining larvae also occur in the *Coleoptera*, or beetles, and in the sawflies, or *Hymenoptera*. The *Lepidoptera* mines are always free of frass, but those of the other insect groups such as fly-miners contain frass along the channels.

The female insect lays her egg either on the surface or inside the leaf. The species that lay eggs on the surface may choose the upper or lower leaf surface. The particular surface used is usually characteristic of the insect species. The egg is cemented onto the leaf by a sticky secretion, and when the larva hatches it burrows its way directly from the egg into the leaf at the point of contact. In the majority of leaf-mining species the egg is inserted inside the leaf tissue by the insect's ovipositor, a special organ which punctures a small hole into the leaf. The hatched larvae pass all their larval life inside the leaf, molting through various stages just as in a free-living caterpillar. Fly larvae pass through three phases, or instars, molting three times, while those of moths molt from four to six times. The larvae produce their characteristic patterns as they hollow out feeding channels. Eventually they pupate, either inside or outside the mine, depending upon the species of insect. During their life inside the leaf they do not eat the outer skin of the leaves since the cuticle is made of material which is hard to digest and offers no nutrition. The insect is also well protected by being under the leaf cuticle.

The various photographs show that there are varied patterns created by the mining activity. Biologists, who like to classify everything, have worked out an elaborate terminology for the different designs. For example, if the bands of a mine track along and around each other, keeping the mine in a small patch of the leaf, it is called a serpentine or heliconome mine because of its resemblance to a snake or spiral. In other species the tracks are not made around each other but are arranged like the coils of an intestine. Hence these are called visceronomes because of their similarity to viscera or intestines. Many other types of mines exist, such as the star-shaped asteronomes. When a mining larva eats out from its source in several different directions it does not produce such a definite geometrical pattern. Instead it produces a "blotch mine" that has the technical name stigmatonome.

Some mining insects lay their eggs only on a certan plant species; others, on a variety of plants. When insects have a particular host-plant preference it is common to find many leaves of the different individual plants with the visiting card of their particular insect predator.

When a leaf is wounded by an insect such as a leaf miner, the injured tissue changes and, to heal the wound, produces callus tissue. In some cases this is accompanied by color changes, hence some mines have spectacular colors. In other cases, insects have made use of the plant's ability to form callus. Callus consists of enlarged cells which have higher water content than normal cells and which are often linked together in chains or threads. It often has minute chloroplasts or none at all, and is therefore much paler in color. The act of egg-laying by the insect stimulates abnormal growth of the spongelike callus tissue. This grows around the insect, forming a case which encloses it; this is called a *gall*. The study of galls, which derives its name from a Greek term, is known as cecidology.

Like the mining cavities, galls are also extremely varied in shape and size, and are often so characteristic of a particular insect as to be useful for its identification.

Some galls may be familiar to you, such as the hairy, sponge-like galls of the wild roses, the bedeguars or rose sponges that are often used as decoratives. The oak apple or oak gall is another well-known one. Galls can be produced by many different organisms that cause trauma to the plant and, consequently, abnormal growth. They are caused mainly by insects laying their eggs in a plant but also by certain algae, fungi, bacteria, or even slime molds. Most leaf galls are insect produced, especially by the gall-flies or Cynipidae. The fly family Cecidonyiidae are another common source of galls. These delicate, two-winged flies produce gall-making gnats and midges.

A most interesting leaf gall in the Amazon forest of Peru occurs in great quantity on the leaves of the tree *Licania cecidiophora*. An unknown insect causes a gall that forms small, doughnutlike rings all over the leaf surface. These are used as beads to form capes and necklaces by the Aguarana Indians. For many years the source of these "beads" of the Jivaro Indian tribe was unknown until ethnobotanist Brent Berlin of the University of California associated them with the leaf galls of the tree.

Another pattern of leaf damage is completely different from the previous ones in that it is much more destructive of the leaf. The tropical forests of Central and South America are full of colonies of *leaf-cutter* ants. These ants are well named since that is exactly what they do. They live in large underground colonies with many chambers and entrances. The worker ants follow specific chemical trails laid down by the ants which lead to a particular tree. They walk in large columns up to the tree and each ant carefully carves out a chunk of leaf considerably larger than itself. The ants then carry the pieces of leaf back along their trail to the nest. It is fascinating to sit and watch these ants laboring ceaselessly along the jungle floor. In an experiment conducted in Quibdó in Colombia, in which we marked some of their leaves with paint, we found that loaded ants traveled one hundred yards in fifty minutes. Since these ants strip all the leaves into shreds from the tree of their choice, they can be serious pests in agricultural land, and are dreaded by tropical farmers.

Why would a colony of ants cart tons of leaves underground so laboriously? It is interesting that they do not eat the leaves they bring. Instead, they deposit them in special underground chambers. These chambers are used to grow fungi on the rotting leaves. The special fungi of the leaf-cutter ants are planted on the leaves by certain ants. The large mass of threadlike fungal structure, or hyphae, increases in mass and forms the food for the ants. The ants are therefore growing large underground fungus gardens to feed themselves. Underground, the fungi form only a mass of threads. Various scientists have grown these fungi in the laboratory to produce their fruiting body or mushroom in order to identify them, since one cannot identify them from the hyphal mass alone. The fungi that the ants use are often specific to a certain species of ant.

Recently scientists have found a new use for this elaborate relationship between ants and rainforest leaves. They found that the ants are selective as to which leaves they choose. It was also discovered that some of the leaves that ants reject and do not collect have chemical substances which are fungicidal. The ants' acceptance or rejection of leaves of certain plant species is now being used as a preliminary indicator of leaves that may contain fungicides of potential use for agriculture. It is hoped that the ants will lead us to new fungicides.

Leaf predators are varied and interesting animals. Instead of regarding them all as pests, we can see that some are even of potential use while others, by their different methods of predation, add to the beauty and fascination of nature around us.

Leaf-perforating insects.

OPPOSITE PAGE: Holes perforated in the leaf of a Melastomataceae near Manaus, Brazil.

ABOVE: Pattern left by the *Cyathula* beetle in Ghana.

BELOW: Mites feeding on a leaf in the West African rainforest.

ABOVE: This symmetrical pattern of leaf perforation is made by a beetle that eats the leaf at the stage when it is folded in bud.

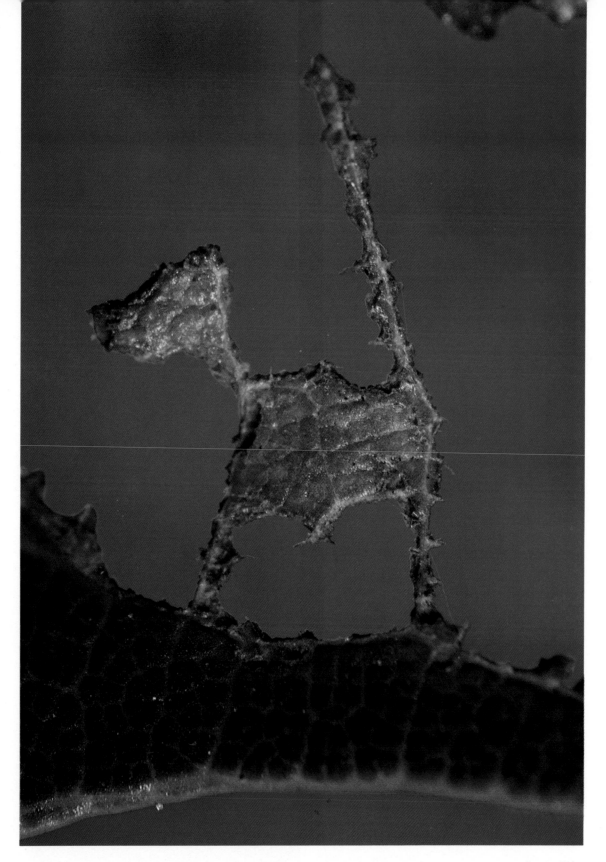

ABOVE: Leaves eaten away by caterpillars sometimes leave strange patterns, such as this "cat."

ABOVE AND RIGHT: Leaf-mining action by an Agromyzidae fly near Manaus, Brazil.

Not all leaf perforations are caused by insects. The leaf patterns of these two members of the jack-in-the-pulpit family (Araceae) are the natural pattern of leaf growth.

OPPOSITE PAGE: A *Caladium* in Brazil.

LEFT: A *Monstera obliqua expilata* from the upper Amazon.

The varied patterns left behind by leaf-mining insects.

ABOVE: Leaf-miner action in Washington, D.C.

LEFT: A leaf in the mountain rainforest in Cibodja, Java.

ABOVE: Mites feeding on leaf in Amazonia.

BELOW: Beetles feeding on a leaf in West Africa.

BELOW: An array of sawfly larvae feeding on a leaf in Ghana.

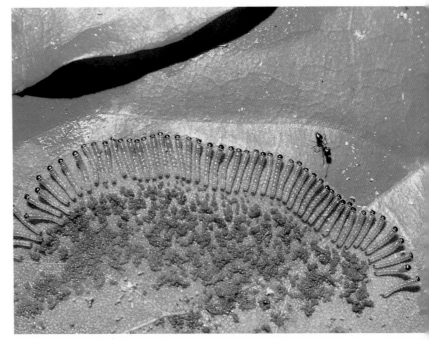

PATTERNS OF LEAF DAMAGE

Skeletonizing leaf eating where the insects leave only the leaf veins.

BELOW AND RIGHT: Leaves skeletonized by beetle larvae in the rain-forest at Manaus, Brazil.

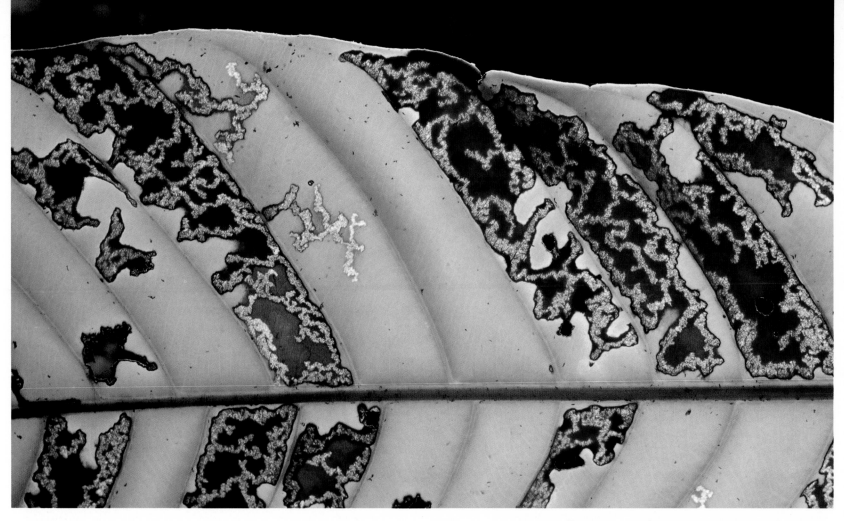

ABOVE: Leaf mining in Sri Lanka by a species of *Acrostrema*.

BELOW: Leaf miner in a broad-leaved forest species of grass (*Pariana* species).

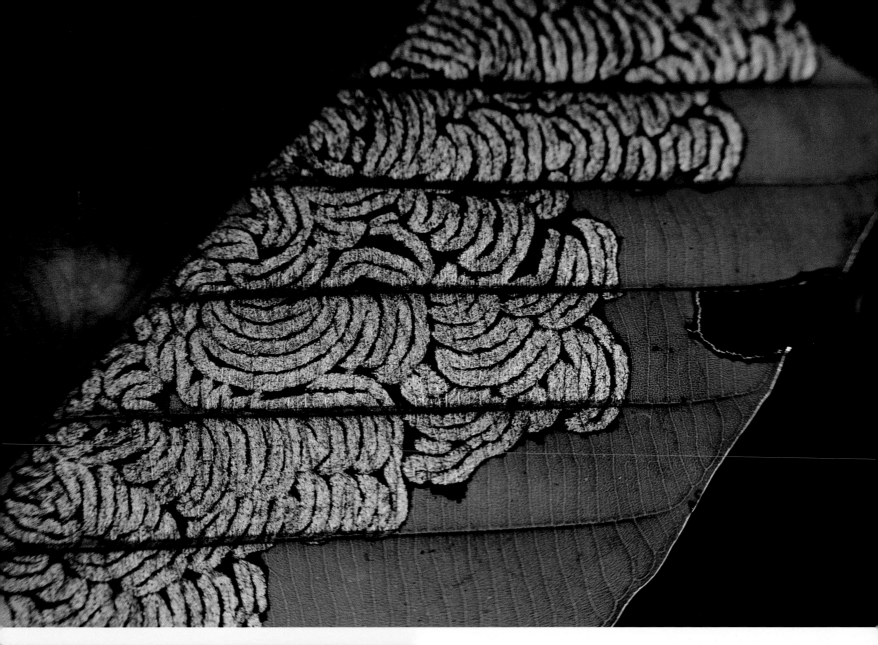

LEFT AND ABOVE: Leaf mining in a visceronome pattern (coiled like an intestine) by a Chrysomelid beetle (*Galerucine* species) in Amazonia.

191

RIGHT: Leaf miners on a leaflet of *Cassia* near Manaus, Brazil.

BELOW: Leaf miners in rainforest on Mount Kinabalu, Sabah.

ABOVE: A leaf being carried by a leaf-cutter ant.

BELOW: A leaf-cutter ant nest near Manaus, Brazil. The worker ants carry in leaf pieces, while the larger soldier ants guard the entrance to the underground nest.

ABOVE: Wax-covered scale insects all facing in the same direction on a leaf on Mount Kinabalu, Sabah.

Useful Leaves

*The leaves and floures of Borage plant into wine
make men and women glad and merry and drive
away all sadnesse dulnesse and melancholy.*

JOHN GERARD,
Herball

*While wormwood hath seed yet a bundle or twain
To save against March, to make flea to refrain,
Where Chamber is swept and wormwood is strown,
No flea for his life dare abide to be known.*

THOMAS TUSSER,
"Five Hundred Points of Good Husbandry"

*How vainly men themselves amaze
To win the Palm, the Oke, or Bayes;
And their uncessant labours see
Crown'd from single Herb or Tree,
Whose short and narrow verged Shade
Does prudently their Toyles upbraid;
While all Flow'rs and all Trees do close
To weave the Garlands of respose.*

ANDREW MARVELL,
"The Garden"

We have already seen the primary use of leaves, that of capturing the sun's energy and carrying out photosynthesis, but people have their own uses of leaves. You can probably compile a long list of useful leaves that play a part in your daily life as food, beverages, and medicines. We have also seen the diversity of leaf structure and form. This diversity both of structure and of chemical constituents, as a defense in response to predation, has also brought about the variety of uses which we humans have for leaves.

Primitive people used leaves as a source of food and shelter and in some cases clothing. Gradually our uses for leaves have become more sophisticated as we have learned more about their structure and contents. The numerous uses to which leaves have been put could fill several books and so we will only mention a few of the many interesting uses of leaves. However, all the useful features have their origin in the evolutionary diversity of plants. Because plants have adapted to so many different environments and predation from different types of animals, one basic leaf form was not sufficient. As a result we can get useful fibers from the huge leaves of the agave, which is adapted to the desert life of Mexico, and in contrast the soft edible leaves of watercress from a plant that is adapted to the aquatic environments of Europe.

Leaves are an important part of our daily diet and help to provide us with necessary vitamins and minerals. In the United States and Europe we are probably most familiar with lettuce and cabbage, which are the most commonly eaten leaves. However, around the world there are a great number of plants with edible leaves.

The lettuce (Lactuca sativa) is a member of the daisy family. The cultivated varieties that we have today look very different from the original wild species. Over thousands of years, through the process of breeding, lettuce has been changed into a more appetizing and juicy leaf. Wild lettuce leaves (Lactuca virosa) have a large amount of milky juice, like a dandelion. The juice is rather bitter and contains a mild narcotic, which was much used by ancient people in folk medicine. The Roman emperor Augustus took lactucarium, the dried sap of wild lettuce, and recovered from a serious illness. He was so grateful that he built an altar to the lettuce plant and a statue to honor it. Today's much more palatable cultivated lettuce does not contain any quantity of narcotic. Many people eat dandelion leaves as a salad. These have a bitter taste which is similar to the primitive lettuce.

The cabbage (Brassica oleracea) is a plant that has been modified through breeding into a remarkable number of forms. The wild species that gave rise to our cabbage grew near the sea, and is a member of the mustard family (Cruciferae). Cultivation of this one species has given rise to many different vegetables: broccoli, brussels sprouts, cabbage, cauliflower, collards, kale, and kohlrabi. In the case of brussels sprouts, cabbage, kale, and kohlrabi it is the leaves that are eaten, but in broccoli and cauliflower it is the modified flowers. This array of different vegetables obtained from one original species shows the potential of plant breeding for the modification of plants. In the United States cabbage is most commonly eaten in the form of cole slaw or sauerkraut, and in Europe it is commonly boiled or used in soup. The Chinese cabbage is a separate species, Brassica campestris, subspecies pekinensis, and is also grown in many different forms.

Cabbages with red leaves are popular in Europe, especially for pickling. The red-leaved type has given rise to ornamental cabbages that are used in gardens as a popular foliage plant.

An important leafy vegetable is spinach (Spinacia oleracea). It belongs to the goosefoot family (Chenopodiaceae) and originally came from Persia. Spinach is particularly popular because of its high content of vitamins and iron. The leaves contain 3.3 percent of iron sesquioxide and are rich in vitamin A. Spinach was introduced to Spain by the Moors and from there its use spread northward throughout Europe.

The common spinach is the most used pot herb, but there are numerous other leaves which are used around the world as a substitute, especially in parts of the world where spinach does not grow well. The Chinese, for example, have numerous spinach substitutes. In the Andean countries and Central America the amaranth has been used for many centuries. While some varieties of amaranth (Amaranthus species) are excellent spinach substitutes, others are becoming increasingly important as a source of cereal grain. In the tropics the quail grass or celosia (Celosia argentea) is another spinach substitute. In China and India the leaves of a species of jute, the jute mallow (Corchorus olitorius), are a popular vegetable.

In several leaf vegetables the leaf stalk, or petiole, is more important than the leaves. The two most commonly eaten petioles are celery and rhubarb. Celery (Apium graveolens) belongs to the carrot family (Apiaceae) and is related to another important leaf which is used as an herb, parsley (Apium petroselinum). Rhubarb (Rheum rhaponticum) was originally considered a medicinal plant, its roots being used as a purgative and for many stomach complaints. Later the succulent petioles were used in pies as a fruit substitute. Its use as a food began in England about 1800. Rhubarb stems contain potassium oxalate, which can poison people susceptible to salts of oxalic acid. People with urinary irritations should also avoid the use of rhubarb. The leaves contain a larger quantity of oxalates and should never be eaten.

Parsley is an ancient herb that comes to us from the Middle East. It was much used by the Greeks and Romans and was first named petroselinum by the Greek scientist Dioscorides. The name was anglicized to petersylinge, then to persele, and eventually to parsley. It is one of the most important seasonings or garnishes used in Europe and America.

Asparagus *(Asparagus officinalis)* does not look very much like a leaf, but the edible part consists of the young shoot buds which are harvested before they open up into feathery plants. These shoots bear scales which are the modified leaves that later fall off. The mature plant bears no leaves, just modified green branches which carry out the photosynthetic function of leaves. The lack of leaves gives away its origin, the desert regions of North Africa, where it was eaten by the Arabs. Asparagus was much esteemed by the Greeks and Romans and the Romans distributed it widely. Pliny mentioned a variety of asparagus in which three heads weighed a pound!

We are also eating leaves when we use the onion *(Allium cepa)*. The bulb is made up of a group of tightly packed scales which are modified leaves. Each scale is fleshy since it is filled with stored nutrients to last over the winter and to produce new leaves and flowers in the spring (see Chapter 16). People have made use of this cache of nutrients for many years. Onions were cultivated by the ancient Egyptians and so are one of the oldest known vegetables. Because of this there has been time to breed many different varieties which vary greatly in color, size, and taste. Onions are grown around the world, mainly in the temperate and subtropical regions but also in the tropics. They are an essential part of the recipes of many national dishes.

Many close relatives of the onion are also important food plants. Garlic *(Allium sativum)* grows in a cluster of bulblets, usually termed cloves, which are actually a group of small bulbs enclosed together by a white skin similar to the segments of an orange. In addition to its popularity as a flavor in the cuisine of many countries, garlic is employed medicinally in many countries. Both garlic and onions were deified by the Egyptians and have a long history of use by the Greeks and Romans. Garlic is frequently mentioned in ancient literature. In Greece, people who ate garlic were prohibited from entry into the temples of the goddess Cybele. The Latin poet Horace detested the smell of garlic and considered its use a sign of vulgarity. Today garlic remains an important ingredient of southern European cooking.

In another species of the onion genus, the leek *(Allium porrum)*, it is more obvious that it is the leaves which are eaten. Leeks are banked up in a similar manner to celery to produce a greater area of white leaf base. Like garlic, the leek was also cultivated in ancient Egypt and was commonly used by the Romans. Pliny records that Emperor Nero ate leeks frequently to clear his voice. The leek is more popular in Britain than America. It is so popular in Wales that it is considered the national plant. On St. David's Day every good Welshman wears a leek.

Many other onion relatives are important and useful plants. The chive *(Allium schoenoprasum)* is one of the most deli-cately flavored of all the onion genus. In the case of chives it is the tender young green leaves that are eaten and enhance many a salad, omelet, or stew.

These are but a few of the many leaves which serve as food around the world. In each region there are leaves used by the local population as a regular part of their cuisine or as a flavor. For example, various South American Indian tribes, many of which are still hunter-gatherers, eat many different forest leaves. To these people leaves, eaten raw or cooked in stews, are an important diet supplement.

So many leaves are used for flavor around the world that it would fill a book just to catalog them. The leaves of many plants contain aromatic compounds which are usually essential oils. The plants have developed their enormous array of these fragrant chemical substances largely as a defense against insect predators. Chemical defense systems have evolved because of the plants' need to minimize the predation by leaf-eating insects. Many of these substances have subsequently been used by people around the world as herbs, spices, and medicines. Examples of leaves which we utilize in this way include bay leaves, parsley, peppermint, sage, and thyme. How dull our food would be without the subtle flavors added by herbs. In the majority of herbs it is the leaves that we use, whereas many of the substances we call spices come from other parts of the plants, such as the roots or the fruit.

The mints are the most familiar flavor leaves to Europeans and North Americans. Although there are many species of mint, three are more commonly used: pennyroyal *(Mentha pulegium)*, peppermint *(M. piperita)*, and spearmint *(M. viridis* or *spicata)*. The latter is the common garden mint usually used in cooking. Mint has long been used and features in much ancient literature. The Latin name *Mentha* is derived from the name of a Greek nymph, Menthe, who according to legend was transformed into the mint plant by Proserpine because of her jealousy of her love for Pluto. Mint was widely used by the Romans who introduced it throughout Europe and into the British Isles, and it was subsequently carried to North America by the Pilgrims. It is featured in a list of plants carried from England to America which was compiled by John Josselyn. He published this in 1672 under the title *New England rarities discovered. . . .* Josselyn, the first person to write a natural history of New England, lived from 1630 to 1675.

We are familiar with mint in our cooking, as a jelly to use with lamb, and as a flavor. It has had thousands of other uses over the centuries. Mint leaves used to be used in baths to perfume the water and, supposedly, to strengthen the nerves. It might seem strange that aromatic substances which we use so much actually evolved in the plant as a protection against predators, yet the mint demonstrates how different creatures react differently to the same smell. Mice cannot stand the smell of mint and will not go anywhere near it. Cottage dwellers in the country have long known that to spread mint leaves along their pantry shelves is the best way to deter mice from raiding their food supplies.

Peppermint is a well-known flavor which also has a long history. The Greeks and Romans both made festive crowns of peppermint, used it in their cooking, and flavored their wine with it. The peppermint flavor used in candies and beverages is made from distilling the volatile oil of peppermint from the leaves. The quality of the oil varies greatly depending upon where the plant is grown. The chief constituent of peppermint oil is menthol, but it has many other substances which add to the subtlety of its flavor, such as cineol, limonene, pinene, and especially menthyl acetate, which gives it the pleasant minty aroma. The peppermint is an important and valuable leaf crop worldwide.

Pennyroyal is a less-known but equally ancient mint that featured as a medicine in the early writings of Dioscorides and Pliny. The latter author tells us that the Roman name was pulegium because of the plant's power to repel fleas (the word for flea in Latin is *pulex*). Pennyroyal is the strongest flavored mint and is rarely used as a food flavor, but is still much used in folk medicine as an antispasmodic and as an emmenagogic.

Many other popular herbs belong to the mint family, which is full of plants with essential oils. Thyme *(Thymus vulgaris)*, one of the most popular, is now cultivated throughout the temperate region for its flavor, derived from the presence of the phenolics thymol and carvacrol. Thyme was formerly spread on the floors of houses to create a pleasant aroma; the name is derived from the Greek word meaning to fumigate. It apparently only became a culinary herb much later in France and Britain, although the Romans used it to flavor cheese and liqueurs.

Bay leaves, often used in cooking as a flavor, come from the bay laurel *(Laurus nobilis)*, a tree native to the Mediterranean region. Its small, shiny leaves were once used to crown heroes and poets. Legend has it that Apollo was wounded by one of Cupid's darts which caused him to fall in love with Daphne, the daughter of a river god. She fled from Apollo to seek her father-god's help. He turned her into a laurel tree. The modern term *bachelor,* used for university degrees, is derived from this same source. It comes from baccalaureate, meaning laurel berry, and came to the English language via the French *bachelier.* Bay leaves contain an aromatic oil containing pinene, geraniol, eugenol, and cineol, which give them their characteristic strong flavor.

Countless other leaves are used around the world as flavors, many of which belong to the same two plant families as the mints and the laurels.

Many of the leaves that have been mentioned above, administered in different ways or different doses, function as medicines. For example, there are many recorded medicinal uses for bay leaves, garlic, peppermint, and spearmint. It is amazing how many different types of plant leaves have been used effectively for med-

icine. Some are used in folk medicine and herbal remedies, while others have entered the modern Western pharmacopoeia. Chinese medicine is based largely on plant products, many of which come from leaves. The leaves of two plants different from the herbs discussed above will serve as examples of medicines extracted from leaves.

The deadly nightshade *(Atropa belladonna)* has long been known both as a medicine and a poison. (Medicines are often toxic substances administered in small doses!) The leaves and roots of this plant contain the alkaloids hyoscyamine and atropine and a small amount of scopolamine. The name *Atropa* is derived from one of the Greek Fates, Atropos, who held the shears to cut the thread of human life. This is obviously a reference to the deadly nature of the plant. The species name *belladonna* is derived from the Spanish for beautiful woman. One property of the chemical constituent of this plant is to dilate the pupils of the eye. It was used by the women of the Spanish court as dilated pupils were considered to be a sign of great beauty. Legends abound for this plant. The soldiers of Macbeth are said to have poisoned the entire invading Danish army with a drink mixed with nightshade which was given to them during peace talks. This enabled Duncan's troops to murder all the sleeping Danes.

It is the atropine and hyoscyamine which give the deadly nightshade its medicinal properties as a narcotic, diuretic, sedative, and antispasmodic. The pupil-dilating property of atropine is made use of by the oculist, who needs only a minute quantity of atropine to dilate pupils while performing eye tests. Atropine extracted from the deadly nightshade and other members of the nightshade family containing the same alkaloid is still an important drug today.

The foxglove *(Digitalis purpurea)* is another plant that is well known for its medicinal properties. Its leaves and seeds contain chemicals called steroids which are heart stimulants. Digitoxin and digitalin have been important drugs in the treatment of certain heart conditions because of their differential effect on the heartbeat. Digitoxin prolongs the period of relaxation of each heartbeat without affecting the contraction. The result is a better blood supply to the heart. The leaves of the foxglove contain approximately 1.25 percent of weight of the useful digitalin. It came into use for heart ailments in the eighteenth century and is mentioned as a remedy for various other ailments in the older herbals. The steroids of the foxglove are very toxic unless used in the small doses needed for their medicinal effect.

All around the world, the leaves of many plants are drunk as teas for medicine and for pleasure. In fact, many of the beverages made from leaves had their origin in folk medicine, for example, tea.

Teas are produced by the infusion of leaves of various herbs and other plants. The ordinary black tea that is drunk by over half of the world's population comes from an Asiatic plant, *Camellia sinensis,* a relative of our garden camellias. The tea leaves that we buy come from the youngest shoots of the plant, which is grown widely in China, India, and Sri Lanka. Tea plants are grown from cuttings. They are allowed to reach about three feet and are then pruned to keep them at a convenient height for harvesting. Leaves for tea come from plucking off the terminal bud and the few leaves below it. This picking stimulates the rapid growth of lateral buds so that the plant can be reharvested every two or three weeks for about ten years.

Black tea is prepared by allowing the freshly picked leaves to wither for a day on racks. The withered leaves are then rolled and spread in cool, moist rooms. Chemical changes take place which turn the leaves to a dark color and give them a fragrant aroma. They are then dried to avoid fungal attack. Different size grades have different names, such as souchong for the largest and pekoe for the next size.

Green tea is prepared by steaming the leaves immediately after picking to prevent the enzyme action that turns the leaves black. It is the favorite type of tea in China and Japan.

Tea contains from 2.5 percent to 4.5 percent caffeine as well as compounds called polyphenolics which contribute to the flavor and also help to cause the black color when they are oxidized. Tea leaves also have a small quantity of an essential oil, theol, which contributes to the aroma.

Many kinds of processing and blending are used to produce the variety of teas available. For example, Earl Gray tea is flavored with bergamot, a product of citrus peel, and Lapsang Souchong has a smoky flavor from a special curing process.

South America has its own native tea, yerba maté, which ranks fourth in consumption among beverages used in the world (next to coffee, tea, and cocoa). It comes from the leaves of a relative of the holly, *Ilex paraguariensis.* This beverage was discovered by the Guarani Indians long before the conquest of South America. The leaf branches are toasted over a fire to dry. These leaves also contain both polyphenolics and caffeine. In Argentina and Paraguay there are elaborate ceremonies attached to the drinking of maté, which is taken through a silver drinking straw. It is used at every meal and frequently between meals. The name maté is derived from the vessel in which the beverage is prepared.

Many leaves are used as smoking material, or fumigants, mostly for their narcotic effect. These effects vary from mild, in the case of tobaccos, to extremely dangerous and intoxicating, in the case of some hallucinogenic leaves.

Tobacco has a long history. Westerners took the plant and the smoking habit to Portugal after discovering the Carib Indians smoking a pipe of peace. From Portugal the Frenchman Jean Nicot introduced it to the rest of Europe. His name was attached to the plant later when the Swedish botanist Linnaeus gave it the scien-

tific name *Nicotiana.* The species *Nicotiana tabacum,* which produces tobacco, is a member of the nightshade family, Solanaceae.

The use of tobacco spread rapidly and became of major economic importance. Tobacco plants are cut at the apex to make the basal leaves grow larger. Different types of tobacco are prepared in different ways. Greater fermentation is used for the darker pipe tobaccos. The stimulant in tobacco is the alkaloid nicotine which decomposes into a number of other substances when smoked, such as pyridine, furfurol, collidine, and hydrocyanic acid. It is these substances that give tobacco its harmful effects. Nicotine is a poison that causes disturbances to the digestive and circulatory organs. Although tobacco leaves are extremely important to the economy of many countries, they should be classified as harmful leaves.

Leaves are useful to people around the world in many other ways. Since early times one of the most important uses of leaves has been for shelter. Many different tribal groups use leaves for making thatch. In the tropics palm leaves are particularly important for thatch, but others are also employed. Leaves often form both the roof and walls of houses. The employment of leaves for shelter must have been one of the first uses of leaves of primitive people. Today, Indians traveling through the jungles of South America will make a shelter of a few wild banana or palm leaves propped up against a stick.

In northeastern Brazil the lower surface of leaves of the carnaúba palm (*Copernicia cerifera*) is covered by a white, waxy substance. This substance is scraped off and collected by the local residents and is melted down to form carnaúba wax, which is one of the most prized waxes for making polishes for automobiles and other products. This useful leaf is one of the few regional products of importance to come from the arid, often drought-stricken area of northeastern Brazil, which caused the explorer Alexander von Humboldt to call it "the tree of life." Various other leaves produce waxes that can be scraped off, but none is superior to that of the carnaúba palm.

Some leaves are used as abrasives. Such leaves are generally hard and sandpaperlike because they have sand grains (silica crystals) in their tissues. In North America the scouring rush (*Equisetum hyemale*) was long used as a pot scrubber and before that by Indian tribes to polish their bows. The well-named sandpaper starwort (*Diplopappus linarifolius*), a common plant of eastern North America in the aster family, has been put to use as a sandpaper to polish horn. In the savannas of South America there is a plant named *Curatella americana* whose leaves feel just like sandpaper to the touch. These leaves are employed by many native groups as both a sandpaper and a pot scrubber. Its local name in Brazil is lixeira, or sandpaper tree.

The leaves of the henna plant (*Lawsonia alba*) have been powdered since early times for use as a hair dye. The practice began in Eastern countries, but since the 1890s henna has been used extensively in Europe mixed with shampoo. Henna is also popular in the Middle East and North Africa to dye fingernails and the manes and hoofs of horses. Henna leaves are an important export of Egypt, Iran, and Turkey.

The leaves of various plants yield fibers of considerable importance. Sisal comes from the leaves of *Agave sisalana* of the plant family Amaryllidaceae, the same family as the daffodil. The enormous leaves of sisal, which grow in a basal rosette, contain tough fibers. The leaves are run through a crusher to scrape off the outer parts and squeeze out the juices. The fibers remain and can be dried and then combed out before being made into rope or fiber bags.

The leaves of a relative of the banana, the abaca *(Musa textilis)*, produce manila hemp. As the name would suggest, this plant is a native of the Philippines, but it is now grown in many tropical areas, such as western Ecuador. The fiber of manila hemp is resistant to salt water and has long been prized by sailors around the world. Fibers from leaves are used for bowstrings by natives in both Africa and South America. The South American Indians use the leaf fibers of the wild pineapple or the tucumá palm *(Astrocaryum tucuma)*, whereas those of Africa use the appropriately named bowstring hemp *(Sanseviera metallica)*, a member of the lily family.

Leaves have long been used for decorative purposes. The Romans used to send leafy branches with gifts to friends at their midwinter Saturnalia festival. The custom was adopted by the early Christians and so evergreens were brought into their houses. The holly *(Ilex aquifolium)* was one of the most popular plants. An old legend tells that the holly first grew under the footsteps where Christ trod on the earth; its thorny leaves and red berries, like drops of blood, are symbolic of Christ's sufferings and crown of thorns. Another plant, the mistletoe *(Viscum album)*, was held in great reverence by the Druids, who went out in white robes carrying golden knives to cut their sacred plant. They used the mistletoe branches to announce the entrance of a new year. The use of mistletoe in homes at Christmas is probably a survival of the use of the Druids' holy plant to protect the possessor from all evil.

Scandinavian legend records that Balder, the god of peace, was killed by an arrow made of mistletoe. He was later resurrected by the other gods and given into the care of the goddess of love. It then became a custom that everyone who passed under the mistletoe should receive a kiss to show that the branch was now an emblem of love rather than hate. Hence the mistletoe and holly leaves have become important adornments of modern holiday homes.

ABOVE: The winged bean *(Psophocarpus tetragonolobus)*, a new miracle crop from the tropics that is native to New Guinea. The pods are edible as well as the beans, it produces a starchlike potato on the root, and its leaves can also be eaten!

USEFUL LEAVES

ABOVE: A locally used spinach of Amazonia, called cariru *(Talinum).*

Hardy greens from China that produce until January are grown experimentally by the Rodale Press in Emmaus, Pennsylvania.

BELOW: An Amazon resident preparing palm leaves to thatch a house. The leaflets are all bent in one direction and then dried before being placed on the roof.

ABOVE: *Celosia argentea,* of the amaranth family, from Sri Lanka is a useful green as a spinach substitute.

RIGHT: A new use as a spinach has been found for the edible leaves of *Celosia,* an attractive plant.

USEFUL LEAVES

LEFT: The abaca species of banana *(Musa textilis)* is grown for the fiber produced by its leaf bases rather than for its fruit. Rope made of abaca is one of the best for marine uses.

BELOW: An herb garden in Greene, Rhode Island, is full of leaves that are harvested for their flavor.

USEFUL LEAVES

ABOVE: The amaranth, a common Andean leaf crop, is grown both for the cereal-like grain and the edible leaves. It can be grown as an annual in cool climates; here it is growing in Pennsylvania.

BELOW: A Paumari Indian from the Amazon demonstrates how to peel off the strips of fiber from the leaf stems of the aruma plant *(Ischnosiphon).*

USEFUL LEAVES

Fossil Leaves: Traces of the Past

Larger still were the various kinds of tree-ferns, the Lepidodedrons and Sigillaria, called club-mosses, though they much resemble palms and cycads. Their stems were ribbed and fluted like Gothic columns, and they grew leaves thickly, tier upon tier, gradually shedding the lowest. And mingled with them were some genuine trees, conifers such as we might recognize today—the first real trees to appear on earth.

JOHN STEWART COLLIS,
The Vision of Glory

We not only have the present-day leaves around us but nature has left traces of its past engraved in stone fossils. The term *fossil,* derived from a Latin word meaning dug up, was coined by the German scientist Georg Agricola in the early sixteenth century. The study of plant fossils is called paleobotany. Paleobotanists have been able to learn a great deal about the past history of the vegetation of the world because of the quantity of fossils deposited in rocks around the world.

Many of the most interesting discoveries have come from the study of leaf fossils because this is the part of the plant that easily becomes fossilized. We are also familiar with fossilized trees and branches such as those found in the Painted Desert of eastern Arizona and now preserved in the Petrified Forest National Park. The park contains the largest known collection of petrified wood in the world. The trees of this area date back to the Triassic period, 200 million years ago, and were buried deeply in mud and sand with volcanic ash. The logs were petrified as the sand was carried into the wood and gradually replaced the wood cells in their original shapes. In later periods the surrounding mud was washed away and the now petrified trees came to the surface. The park of almost 100,000 acres is one of the treasures of botanical history.

Leaves often fossilized when they fell to the bottom of a pond and became covered with mud and sand in an oxygen-free environment where decay could not take place. Gradually they became buried deeper and deeper, and under greater weight from above and over millions of years the sediments became stones. The leaf tissues, just as in the case of the petrified woods, were slowly replaced by minerals. The process is so gradual that often even the cellular structure of leaves is preserved. In addition to leaves, fossil flowers and fruit are often found, and with this record preserved in stone, paleobotanists are able to reconstruct the geological, climatological, and vegetational happenings of the past.

Another way in which leaves and other plant parts have been fossilized is in amber. Amber is fossilized resin, usually of pines, that was produced by ancient plants. It hardened together with any leaves, insects, and other things that settled in it. Items that have been preserved in amber show some of the best structural details of any fossil. Amber was a barter item of Neolithic man about 5,000 years ago. It became an important item of trade and even of worship in many primitive societies, and was traded far from its main source in the region of the Baltic Sea. It was prized by both the Greeks and the Romans. In the fourteenth century, the Ritten-order of knights claimed exclusive ownership of amber and the hoarding of it was punished by hanging. The order formed guilds of amber turners and conducted sales all over Europe. Today amber is used in jewelry and in varnishes. Besides the Baltic source, it was found in various other places such as some of the Caribbean Islands. Much of the paleobotanical history that is contained has been lost because so much amber has been broken up and used. Some of the fossilized insects found in amber belong to extinct species.

Fossils are also found in asphalt and coal deposits and the latter often have good impressions of leaves.

Fossils with leaf-bearing plants begin to appear in deposits of the Devonian period, almost 400 million years ago. At that time there were only relatively simple plants that today we would call primitive. The fossil record shows that the club mosses and the horsetails predominated as land plants. Today only the genus *Equisetum* survives from the Equisetophyta, which was a large group of primitive vascular plants of great importance in the Devonian and Carboniferous periods. Horsetails have small, scalelike leaves around a hollow, jointed stem. The stem is green and carries out photosynthesis; the scales are brown and papery. The scouring rush, *(Equisetum hyemale),* described in chapter 20, was a plant of this group. Today most Equisetums are small plants. Only the giant *E. giganteum* of South America reaches about thirty feet in height.

By the time of the Carboniferous period, some 300 million years ago, the horsetails reached gigantic heights and the many treelike ones must have given a bizarre appearance to the landscape. The Carboniferous was the period of horsetails and ferns. It gets its name from the fact that the coal deposits of the world were formed at that time. The luxuriant growth and the warm climate together with the large quantity of bogs caused great quantities of peat to form. As the peat became covered with the weight of sediments, it gradually turned into lignite and then coal. The pressure of the sediments above forced out much of the water and caused volatile compounds to escape, and the nonvolatile carbon material gradually metamorphosed into the hard mass of coal. Since much of the world's coal was formed in the Carboniferous period, most of it is composed of ferns and horsetails. However, coal was also formed later in the Permian through the Tertiary periods.

Coal deposits contain carbonized stems, leaves, seeds, and even whole tree stumps which can be clearly seen in the softer types of coal. This coal, one of the main reserves of fossil fuel in the world, originated from the leaves and stems of the plants which covered the land surface of our planet about 240 million years ago. Since so many leaves are preserved in coal it is a wonderful source of information about the history of vegetation.

Following the Carboniferous period, the Permian period began about 280 million years ago. During that time the world's climate became drier and less swamp was formed and consequently less coal. The tree horsetails and ferns still abounded, but the conifers had begun to increase. The maidenhair trees or ginkgos began to flourish and reached their peak by 150 million years ago in the Jurassic period. The ginkgo *(Ginkgo biloba)* is a "living fossil" since one species managed to survive until today in remote areas of China, where it was planted outside temples as a sacred tree. It has become a popular street tree in the United States, which has increased the possibility of its continued survival. The ginkgo produces trees with the separate sexes on different trees (dioecious). The male trees are preferred in cultivation as a street tree because of the unpleasant smell of the pulp that surrounds the seed in the female tree. However, in China and Japan, the seed of the ginkgo is a popular food item. The most interesting fact about the ginkgo is that the leaves of fossils exactly resemble the leaves of living plants. Over millions of years the form of the leaf has not changed at all, as the photograph shows.

Other cone-bearing trees that began to prosper in the Permian period were the cycads, a group that also survives mostly in the tropics of the Old World, and the pines. The pines, unlike most of the other groups of the Permian period, have continued to flourish right up to the present day. The seed fern *Glossopteris* made a rapid spread over the southern hemisphere during the Permian period. The fossil record shows its wide distribution in South America, Antarctica, Australia, and South Africa, adding to the evidence that these continents were all joined into the single larger land mass of Gondwanaland at that time. A plant is unlikely to have been able to spread over sea water between separated continents.

The Permian period was followed by the Mesozoic age, which began 225 million years ago and is divided into three periods: Triassic, Jurassic, and Cretaceous. The great horsetails and club mosses rapidly declined in the Mesozoic, but ginkgos and tree ferns continued to abound. The *Sequoia* trees began to appear and continued to be widespread in the northern hemisphere around the world until the Ice Age of the Quaternary period reduced their distribution to the relics that remain in the western United States.

The Jurassic period, which was the age of the dinosaurs, was dominated by the presence of cycads, while conifers, ginkgos, ferns, and horsetails still abounded. During the last period of the Mesozoic, the Cretaceous, a sudden change took place and flowering plants were abundant. Beech, magnolia, and sassafras were common. By the end of the period, 65 million years ago, many present-day groups of plants—birches, elm, laurels, maples, and oaks—were dominant. The grasses were also plentiful. It was during the late Jurassic and early Cretaceous periods that the broad leaves of the angiosperms or seed plants began to appear and the deciduous habit developed.

Although the fossil record shows the rapid expansion of these angiosperms, it does not show us exactly where they come from. The origin of the seed plants is still much debated. Their fossils begin to appear sporadically in the early Cretaceous period, but they were obviously outnumbered by ferns and gymnosperms. By the end of the Cretaceous the seed plants had become dominant.

One of the most spectacular finds of fossil leaves in recent years was reported by scientists Karl J. Niklas and David E. Giannasi while they were employed at the New York Botanical Garden. In the paleobotany collection there they found species collected in 1968 by an amateur paleobotanist, Bake Young. These fossil specimens of leaves from Succor Creek, Oregon, were 25 million to 30 million years old, yet still had green leaves. In this case, the actual leaves had become preserved rather than a replacement of cells

by minerals as in the case in most leaf fossils. Leaves of the hackberry *(Celtis)*, elm *(Ulmus)*, and Japanese elm *(Zelkova)* were found.

Giannasi and Niklas were able to make a detailed study of the chemistry and anatomy of these leaves. They analyzed the components of chlorophyll and isolated more than fifty different chemical substances, such as fatty acids, steroids, hydrocarbons, and flavonoid pigments. This was a remarkable opportunity to learn if any changes in such complicated structures as chlorophyll had evolved over the 30 million-year interval. Their comparison of the chemistry of the leaves of each species with their nearest living relative showed that subtle chemical differences existed between the fossil genera and their living relatives.

How could leaves be so perfectly preserved for 30 million years as to have even maintained their green color? These fossils are preserved in a fine-grained clay called schmectite which is water repellant and consists of coalesced volcanic ash. The ash came from now-extinct volcanoes of the Columbia River plateau. The fine grain of the ash and its water-repellant properties explain why the pigments were not leached out of the leaves. Giannasi and Niklas, however, performed laboratory experiments, packing leaves in volcanic ash and heating them to determine at what temperature the pigment would be destroyed. They concluded that at above 74° C the pigments would have deteriorated and the leaves would not have been preserved. While lava is extremely hot, volcanic ash can be relatively cool (64° C) by the time it settles on the ground. Therefore these green fossils were formed where plant leaves became rapidly buried in warm, fine volcanic ash. The warm ash, due to its particulate nature, acted as a dessicant and the leaves were quickly dehydrated, in a process rather similar to freeze-drying. This prevented rot by microorganisms, and the most perfect of all leaf fossils were preserved to tell us 30 million years later what prehistoric leaves were like. Subsequently, Niklas and Giannasi even found leaves with fall coloration in the same deposits, and also discovered leaves of both maples and oaks which were analyzed chemically and found to differ little from extant species. They were able to show that little flavonoid and steroid evolution has occurred in these species since the time these fossils were formed.

Fossil leaves are useful for giving us a general idea of the development of the early flora. Early paleobotanists overemphasized the comparison of fossil leaves with modern leaves, which led to many false conclusions. Nevertheless, the fossils still reveal the history of modern-day plants.

Today paleobotanists are building up a large reference collection of modern leaves for comparison with their fossils. For this type of study the venation patterns are particularly important; therefore, techniques which show them are preferred. It is common to treat leaves chemically so that they become bleached and cleared. In this transparent form, the veins show up clearly. The cleared leaves are then stained to bring out the vein patterns. These are then much more readily comparable with the fossil leaves, in which venation is the most easily observed characteristic.

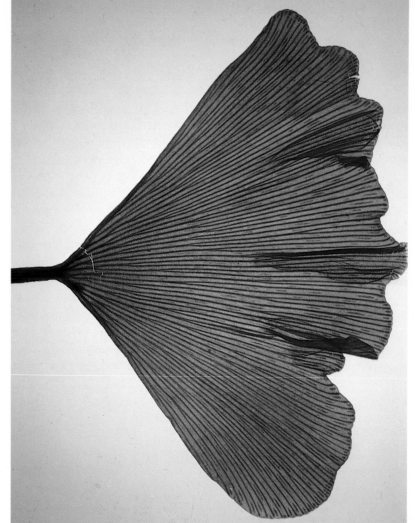

ABOVE: The leaf of the maidenhair tree, *Ginkgo biloba*, photographed in eastern China, where the living fossil survived as a sacred plant.

TOP RIGHT: A ginkgo leaf, cleared and stained for comparison with fossils in the paleobotany laboratory of the Smithsonian Institution.

BOTTOM RIGHT: A fossil palm leaf.

ABOVE: Fossils of the ginkgo tree show that its ancient leaf form is exactly similar to the living trees of today.

LEFT: A fossil palm tree.

The extraordinarily preserved 30 million-year-old fossil leaves from Succor Creek, Oregon, that preserved their coloration and structure and were studied by scientists Giannasi and Niklas.

BELOW: A fossil *Zelkova* leaf removed from its volcanic matrix. Note the impression of the underside of leaf in the matrix. (Photo by Ralph Rocklin, courtesy D. Giannasi)

ABOVE: An autumn-colored fossil leaf peeling off its silt matrix.

The Mimicry of Leaves by Insects

When we see leaf-eating insects green, and bark feeders mottled-grey; the alpine ptarmigan white in winter, the red-grouse the colour of heather, and the black-grouse that of peaty earth, we must believe that these tints are of service to these birds and insects in preserving them from danger.

CHARLES DARWIN,
On the Origin of Species

Nature's camouflage is perfect! Some of the hardest types of insects to find in the Amazon forest are those which mimic leaves. The forest is full of these incredible insects, but they can be spotted only when they move. One can be staring at a tree branch two feet away and be completely oblivious of the fact one of the "leaves" is really an insect. There are mimics that copy all types of leaves found in the forest. There are dead-leaf insects, green ones, and even red ones that resemble the young leaves that were described in Chapter 6. There are look-alikes for twigs, tree bark, leaf stalks, leaves damaged by leaf miners and other predators, or even moths that look just like bird droppings on a leaf.

Mimicry is a common biological phenomenon. In Chapter 7 we saw how a poisonous organism is often mimicked by a harmless one. This Batesian mimicry of one insect by another is an effective way of avoiding predators. An equally efficient disguise is for the insect to blend into the background so perfectly that a bird will never see it. The only difficulty comes in moving from place to place.

It is easy to see how these camouflage patterns evolved. An insect that resembled a leaf slightly more than another stood a greater chance of survival. Gradually the poorly hidden insects were eliminated by bird predators and the camouflaged ones survived. As this process continued over thousands of years and many generations the disguise has become progressively more perfect, so that today we have moths with wings that resemble the leaf veins of plants and katydids that look exactly like twigs.

The Industrial Revolution of nineteenth-century Britain affords us an example of how camouflage can occur. The peppered moth was a light-gray color with a pattern of darker spots and stripes. It blended well with the bark of birch trees and was little preyed upon. In the 1850s the new industries of Midland England changed the color of the tree barks with their smoke pollution. The light-colored moths began to stand out well against the background of the dark trees and were an easy target for predatory birds. Fortunately for the peppered moth, there was a tendency for occasional individuals to be a darker color. This phenomenon of melanism, as it is called, produced moths that were well hidden against the new background of soot-polluted trees. In time the whole population of the peppered moth changed its color to the darker variety because now the darker ones survived while the light ones were eaten by the birds. For a while it was possible to find only dark moths. Today, with the recent cleanup of pollution, the tide is turning and it is again common to see light peppered moths well disguised against unpolluted tree trunks. This changeover has been in effect a laboratory to demonstrate the evolution of camouflage in insects; indeed, this particular case is known as industrial melanism.

The wonderful examples of nature's camouflage shown in the photographs have evolved because in nature the insect that looks least conspicuous is likely to survive and breed the next generation. This survival of the fittest or the best-adapted individuals is the way in which evolution has come about. Since leaves abound in the tropical forest whether they are green and on the trees or brown and on the ground, one of the most perfect ways to hide is to resemble a leaf. The amazing thing is that so many different groups of insects have evolved this same system. They have copied many of the available leaf forms and conditions so that there is now a tremendous diversity of leaf mimics in the tropical

rainforests of the world. Patience is required to study or to photograph these remarkable animals because they are often difficult to find.

BELOW: This Notodontidae moth *(Antaea jaraguana)* from Manaus, Brazil, has a wing pattern that exactly resembles a dead leaf and its venation.

ABOVE: A Geometridae moth *(Oxydia yema)* from Venezuela also mimics dead leaves.

TOP RIGHT: A Notodontidae moth (*Hemiceras* species) from Amazonia resembles a young red leaf.

MIDDLE RIGHT: A Pyralidae moth from Costa Rica (*Boccharis obliqualis*) resembles a leaf damaged by leaf miners.

BOTTOM RIGHT: The Lasiocampidae moth, *Euglyphis claudia*, from Manaus, Brazil, is difficult to spot on a leaf undersurface of the same color.

ABOVE: This Arctiidae or tiger moth (*Evius albiscripta*) from Manaus, Brazil, resembles a damaged leaf.

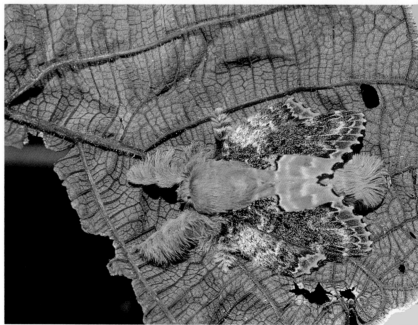

THE MIMICRY OF LEAVES

TOP LEFT: A bird dropping on a leaf for comparison with the *Rifargia* moth's disguise.

MIDDLE LEFT: The Notodontidae moth *Rifargia causia* resembles a bird dropping on a leaf.

BOTTOM LEFT: A Tortricidae moth from Java mimics old leaves.

ABOVE: The Arctiidae moth *Thyractia cedo-nulli* from Manaus, Brazil, has a perfect camouflage of old, damaged leaves.

BELOW: The Ctenuchidae moth *Eucereon confusum* from Manaus, Brazil, with its leaf-damage disguise.

TOP LEFT: This Ithomiidae butterfly gets its camouflage by having completely transparent wings.

BOTTOM LEFT: A Noctuidae moth from Belém, Brazil, that is hard to spot against a tree trunk.

TOP RIGHT: A katydid in a cryptic position on a leaf at Tingo Maria, Peru.

BOTTOM RIGHT: Resembling a twig is another good camouflage, as seen in this Tettigoniidae (*Paraphidnia* species) from Venezuela.

ABOVE: This crowned katydid (*Markia hystrix*) from Venezuela is feeding on a lichen which it matches.

LEFT: This butterfly caterpillar is well concealed from predators while it lies along a leaf stalk.

ABOVE: A well-hidden moth of the Noctuidae.

TOP RIGHT: A katydid (*Steirodon* species) resembles a green leaf; seen near Manaus, Brazil.

MIDDLE RIGHT: This is not a twig but a moth of the Saturniidae family (*Loxolomia serpentina*) from Manaus, Brazil.

BOTTOM RIGHT: This amazingly patterned katydid (*Pychnopalpa* species) is an exact mimic of a damaged leaf.

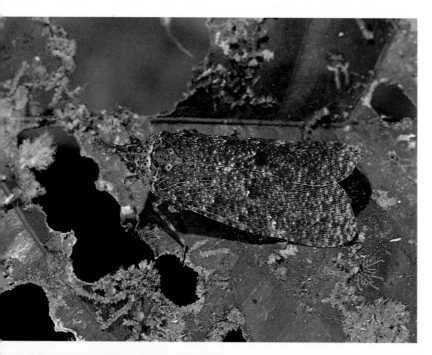

LEFT: A well-camouflaged plant hopper insect (Fulgoridae) on a leaf in Amazonian Brazil.

BELOW: This orchid flower from Colombia, *Lepanthes calodictyon*, imitates an insect in a reverse situation.

ABOVE: A moth of the Notodontidae family, *Hapigia gaudens*, which blends into its Amazon forest background.

LEFT: This *Hemiceras* moth is a realistic copy of a dead leaf.

TOP LEFT: This moth's disguise is to resemble a partly eaten leaf.

BOTTOM LEFT: This Notodontidae moth, *Antaea juturna,* is a leaf mimic.

BELOW: A West African hawk moth, *Euchloron megaera,* which blends well with the leaves on which it rests.

CHAPTER 23

The Herbarium and Leaf Collecting

A herbarium is a museum collection of dried, pressed plant material which has been mounted on cards and filed. The herbaria of the world vary from small private collections of only a few specimens to large, multimillion-specimen public herbaria such as those of the Royal Botanic Gardens in Kew, England, and the Komarov Botanical Institute in Leningrad, Russia, each with more than 5 million specimens, or The New York Botanical Garden with 4.3 million specimens.

During the early sixteenth century Italian botanists Luca Gini, Andrea Caesalpini, and others realized that plants could be dried and pressed to serve as a good reference collection from which other plants could be identified. Once initiated, the practice of making herbaria spread rapidly throughout Europe and on to anywhere in the world where plants were being studied. Today there are 1,729 public herbaria cited in the current *Index Herbariorum,* which lists the herbaria of the world. These herbaria contain more than 180 million specimens, an invaluable resource for the study of the vegetation of the world.

Many famous botanists built up herbaria of their own or for their institutions and all systematic botanists collect specimens for their studies. Herbarium specimens were collected by such people as Carl von Linné or Linnaeus, the founder of biological nomenclature, and Charles Darwin, the discoverer of evolution. Botanists were sent to collect specimens on many of the early discovery expeditions around the world. For example, on the first voyage of Captain Cook (1768–1771) on the ship *H.M.S. Endeavour*, botanists Sir Joseph Banks and Daniel Solander were the collectors, and specimens were collected by William Clark on the Lewis and Clark expeditions in 1804–1806 that opened up the way to the northwestern United States.

Based on the plants he collected and those which other people sent to him, Linnaeus named about 10,000 species. His great contribution to science was the creation of the binomial system of nomenclature whereby every organism is given two Latin names, the first indicating the genus to which it belongs and the second the species name within the genus. For example, the plum is named *Prunus domestica* L. and the cherry, another species in the same genus, is *Prunus cerasus* L., while the peach is *Prunus persica* (L.) Batsch. The apple, on the other hand, belongs to another genus, *Malus*, and is called *Malus sylvestris* Mill. Both genera belong to the large rose family, Rosacaeae, and are grouped together in that family. The L. after the name refers to Linnaeus, the botanist who first described the species. All plant names cite the authors in this way in technical literature.

Linnaeus also created a system of classification, largely based on the number of flower parts, which served to group organisms together and to stimulate interest in classification. His classification is now considered outdated and artificial because it did not group related species together. Modern systems of classification consider the evolutionary relationships of organisms. Whereas Linnaeus's classification soon became outdated, his binomial nomenclatural system has withstood the test of time. Scientists and other people using plants or animals have realized the advantage of having a single, international, Latin name which does not vary from country to country or even regionally within a single country. For example, the plant with the scientific name *Daucus carota* L. is called Queen Anne's lace in New England and wild carrot in Britain, but to scientists it has just the universal Latin name.

A good herbarium specimen consists of the leaves of a plant together with attached flowers or fruit. In the case of small herbs the entire plant may be used but in the case of trees or shrubs it will be a branch with flowers and leaves. To be preserved a specimen must be completely dried because it will rot if left humid. Professional botanists use many different methods of drying specimens, but they all involve pressing the specimen between paper (usually used newspaper) with blotters next to the paper and corrugated cardboard or aluminum between the blotters. This allows the circulation of air and thus promotes drying rather than rotting. In humid climates artificial heat is needed; in dry climates specimens can be dried by daily change of newspapers and drying the

blotters in the sun. This usually works well but one of the authors of this book was collecting in Turkey and a twister came through the camp and blew away all the blotters which were drying in the sun! To the delight of the local children it was necessary to employ about twenty of them for the remainder of the day to retrieve blotters from all over the town of Eğridir!

A herbarium specimen is also accompanied by a label with notes by the collector giving details of the habitat where the plant grew and the flower's color—because the original color may not be preserved. Earlier collectors often did not realize the importance of this documentation, but more recent collections record all of this essential information. Many collectors have also noted the uses of plants which they collect so that there is a wealth of information about potential uses of plants stored on the specimen labels of the plants of the world. Ethnobotanist Siri von Reis considered this so important that she formed a team which compiled all the uses of plants recorded over centuries in the more than 4 million specimen herbaria of Harvard University and The New York Botanical Garden. The resulting books from this study give us hints of where to look in the plant kingdom for new medicines, food plants, fibers, and many other potential applications of the world's flora.

You are probably asking why it is necessary to accumulate so many specimens of the world's flora in so many different herbaria. The herbarium is the basic tool used to define and identify the approximately 300,000 species of vascular plants that inhabit our planet. Fundamental to any use of plants is the existence of a system of classification so that they can be identified and referred to systematically. If a plant is discovered in the Amazon rainforest which contains a new drug, it is necessary to have a system of classification whereby someone can go back and find the same plant again. The existence of a herbarium specimen as a basic reference enables such a process to occur. When a new species of plant is collected and named, a herbarium specimen, called the type specimen, is selected as an example of that species. Future workers can then go back to that specimen to find out to what each name referred. For example, the types of many of the plants described by Linnaeus are housed in the herbarium of the Linnean Society of London. Because specimens are long-lasting when properly cared for, it is still possible to study these collections and compare them with modern collections.

The herbarium tells us much more than the correct name or the use of a particular plant. It is a source of information about the distribution or geography of the plants of the world. For this reason there are many duplicate specimens of each species in herbaria. It is important to know the range of each species as well as the ecological details, such as in which habitat it occurs. If a tree is found to have useful timber in one local region, the herbarium specimens can answer the question as to where else the species grows and are thus providing useful information for the forester. The wealth of data stored in herbaria are vital for foresters, agriculturists, conservationists, pharmaceutical companies, and many other users of plants. The study of poisonous plants, medicinal plants, plant fibers, and hundreds of other plant products involves the consultation of the herbarium. Anyone who needs to identify a plant for any purpose either uses a herbarium directly for comparison or uses a monograph or field guide which was based on an extensive herbarium study.

Chemists have found another use for the herbarium—that of chemical study of the plants. Tiny fragments of the leaves, the removal of which does not change the specimen, can be subjected to chemical analyses to determine the constituents of the plant. This provides extra evidence for use by the taxonomist in classification, or it can be used to look for potentially useful compounds. Only the more stable compounds, such as many alkaloids, will survive the drying and pressing process. Some can last an extremely long time. For example, tests showed that a leaf of coca (*Erythroxylum coca*) found with a 1,500-year-old mummy in Peru still contained the cocaine alkaloids.

You may want to collect herbarium specimens for yourself or perhaps make just a leaf collection to demonstrate the fascinating variety of leaves. This can be a most interesting hobby, but keep in mind the fact that some plants are very rare and consequently should never be collected. Never collect a whole plant when it is rare or endangered or if you can only find a single one growing. The collection of leaves will obviously do less harm to the plants.

Specimens of leaves must be carefully dried by placing them between sheets of newspaper with a weight on top to press them flat. Place corrugated cardboard between each specimen. This can easily be cut to the size of the paper from a cardboard box. The resulting stack of plants between newspaper and corrugates should then be placed in a warm place to dry. If artificial heat is not used the newspapers should be changed daily until they no longer absorb moisture from the leaves of the plant. Generally the quicker you dry your leaves the better they will retain their original color.

Dried specimens can then be mounted on white cards. The standard herbarium size in the United States is 11½ × 16 inches, but leaf collections can be mounted on much smaller cards. Do not forget to leave space in the lower right-hand corner for a label which records the field notes.

The best glue to use is a white glue such as Elmer's. Do not use Scotch tape because it quickly deteriorates with age and also hides part of the plant. Glue should be spread evenly over one side of the leaves and then the leaves pressed down flat onto the card. Leave a weight of some sort on top of them for fifteen minutes to ensure that they are firmly and evenly stuck to the card. Professional herbaria are always careful that not all leaves are glued

down with the same side up so that both surfaces appear for future study. It is annoying to find that a specimen has been mounted in such a way that only the upper surface appears, when it is critical to look at the hairs on the lower surface. For a leaf collection you will find it interesting to observe the differences between the two surfaces.

If you are collecting leaves for ornamental purposes there are many potential ways in which they can be exhibited. Arrangements of leaves and flowers can be mounted on cardboard and then framed in a single picture frame. This can make an elegant decoration or gift for a friend. Many leaf collectors make note cards or greeting cards from pressed plants. Use your artistic ability to arrange the specimens on your picture. The use of different colored cardboard can be used to create different effects and to emphasize the various characteristics of leaves.

If you can keep either a herbarium or a leaf collection, be sure to avoid infestation by insects. When neglected, a herbarium can be completely destroyed by insects. This can be prevented by the use of mothballs in a container where you keep your specimens.

People often comment that they would like to preserve the fall colors of leaves to decorate the house, to frame, to add to flower arrangements, or to use them on cards. There are various methods to preserve leaves; different ways work better for different plants.

Try placing a freshly cut fall branch indoors somewhere cool such as the basement and just allowing it to dry out. This method works well for oaks and beeches. If it does not work, split the stem of a branch and place it in a jar with a solution of water (one part) and glycerin (four parts) for two weeks.

Individual leaves are often easily preserved by coating them with paraffin wax. Wax is melted in a pan and the leaves are dipped. Care should be taken to produce only a thin coating of wax so as to avoid obscuring the color of the leaf. One of the best modern methods is by embedding them in plastic. This method can be used to produce paperweights or other decorative objects.

One of the best ways to preserve fall color, which works for some of the hardest-to-preserve species, involves the use of sand. Prepare a wooden box and cover the bottom with sand to the size of the branch you wish to preserve. Next suspend the branch inside the box, laid on top of the sand, and support it with wire or sticks. Heat up a pan of sand until it is almost too hot to touch and then pour this carefully over the branch until it is covered. The warm sand will dry out and the leaves will be nicely pressed. Take care to arrange the leaves in the desired positions as the sand is poured gradually into the box.

One of the ways in which one of the authors collects leaves (and flowers) is on postage stamps. There are so many stamps around the world that illustrate plants that it is an excellent way of learning about the flora of far away places. A small selection of

Some of the leaf features described in this book can be found on the postage stamps of the world.

The stipular spines of *Acacia drepanolobium* (Uganda).

The simple alternate leaves of a species of *Protea* (Zaire).

The spathe of an aroid, *Zantedeschia aethiopica* (South Africa).

The pineapple, a bromeliad (Costa Rica).

A common species of the savannas of central Brazil, *Palicourea rigida* in the coffee family, which has thick, leathery leaves characteristic of many savanna species (Brazil).

The Amazonian royal water lily, *Victoria amazonica*, with its large floating leaves (Rumania).

The imparipinnate (odd-pinnate) compound leaf of *Connarus griffonianus* (Congo).

The leaves of most cacti are reduced to spines, as in this *Coryphantha vivipara* cactus (Poland).

The showy bracts of the bird-of-paradise flower, *Strelitzia reginae* (Poland).

The imparipinnate compound leaves of *Sophora alopecuroides* (Mongolia).

The simple alternate leaves of *Clappertonia ficifolia* (Dahomey).

The Hawaiian wild broadbean showing the compound leaves, the stipules, and the tendrils (United States).

The sea holly *(Eryngium)* with its prickly leaves (Poland).

The delicate leaves of chamomile *(Matricaria chamomilla),* a useful medicinal herb (East Germany).

The compound leaf of *Millettia laurentii* (Congo).

The leaves of *Azalea pontica,* an ornamental plant (Poland).

The variegated leaves of the wild cyclamen, *Cyclamen europaeum* (Hungary).

The spinous cactus *Ferocactus glaucescens* (Rumania).

The variegated leaves of a bromeliad, *Vriesea* species (Belgium).

The digitate leaves of *Dentaria glandulosa* (Hungary).

Some interesting herbarium specimens from the herbarium of The New York Botanical Garden.

BELOW: This specimen of *Thibaudia mellifera* was collected in Peru by Hipolito Ruiz and José Pavon between 1777 and 1788 and remains in excellent condition.

ABOVE: A historic specimen, collected by the pioneer of North American botany Asa Gray in Watertown, New York, in 1834, and still in good condition.

RIGHT: An early collection made by Scottish botanist and explorer David Douglas from California, which is the type of the species *Nemophila insignis* described from this collection in 1835.

OPPOSITE PAGE: Some leaves are hard to press. This long leaf of a seaweed is mounted in a series of joined sheets.

HERBARIUM AND LEAF COLLECTING

ABOVE: The type specimen of a new species discovered in 1965. This *Saccifolium bandeirae* proved also to be a new family of flowering plants which was described by its collector, Bassett Maguire.

LEFT: A specimen collected by William Clark in Oregon on the Lewis and Clark Expedition remains well preserved in the herbarium of The New York Botanical Garden.

HERBARIUM AND LEAF COLLECTING

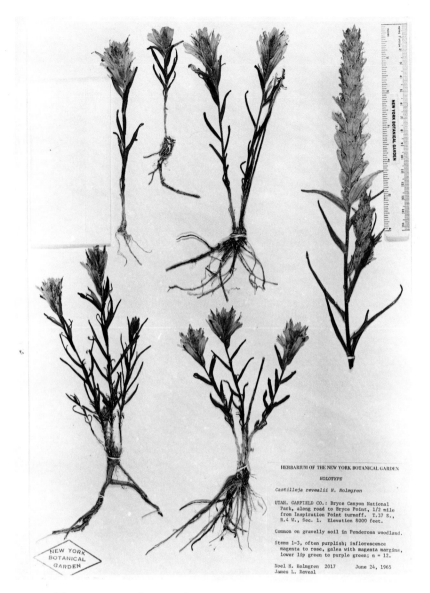

ABOVE: The type specimen of *Castilleja revealii,* a new species discovered in Utah in 1965.

ABOVE: A general view of part of the 4.5 million specimen herbarium of The New York Botanical Garden, one of the largest in the United States.

The Method of Clearing and Staining Leaves

The simplest method of clearing and staining leaves to observe the details of venation or skeleton is as follows:

1. Submerge leaves in a 5 percent solution of sodium hydroxide (NaOH).
2. Change solution daily until leaf is cleared.
3. In order to stain, the leaves must now be dehydrated, using gradually increasing solutions of alcohol. Place in 50 percent alcohol for at least six hours, followed by 80 percent, 90 percent, and 100 percent.
4. Submerge in 2 percent saffranin solution and the skeleton will take up the color.

A leaf prepared in such a way can then be mounted on a glass slide after it has been washed with xylol. It should be mounted with Canada balsam and covered with a cover slip.

The photographs of cleared leaves in this book were prepared by this method. In some cases where leaves are thick and hard to clear, hydrochloric acid (HCl) is better than sodium hydroxide.

How to Enjoy Leaf Variation Through Leaf Prints

Leaf prints are made directly from plants, and can be a very rewarding way of permanently recording leaf variation. If you decide to make one you will be following a technique used about 1490 by Leonardo da Vinci, who printed a sage leaf with a paint of lamp-black mixed with oil. This print is included in the *Codex Atlanticus,* as was discussed by Frank Anderson of The New York Botanical Garden in an article in *Garden Journal* (April 1971). There is even a whole book of leaf prints called *The Leaf Book* by Ida Geary (A. Philpott, Tamal Land Press, Fairfax, California, 1972), a most useful field guide to the leaves of the plants of northern California.

If you would like to try to make a leaf print you will need only some black-printing ink (black is best), a brush, and some stiff, white rice paper. The plant should be spread out on newspapers and brushed evenly with ink (you can use either water-soluble or oil-based ink). Be careful to spread the ink evenly without large drops in any place. Place the plant on a clean part of the newspaper and then place the rice paper over the ink plant and press down firmly. Press and rub the paper gently to make the imprint on the rice paper, then remove the rice paper and turn it with the ink side up to dry. It is important to have the plant lying flat before starting the print or else movement will smudge the ink. It is therefore best to press the plant flat first under the weight of a thick book. Try this on a few different leaves and learn the variety of patterns you can make from the amazing diversity of leaves. You can use everything from delicate maidenhair ferns or Queen Anne's lace to large oak or maple leaves. The leaf prints for this book were made by the teenage daughter of one of the authors, Sarah E. Prance.

LEAF VARIATION THROUGH PRINTS

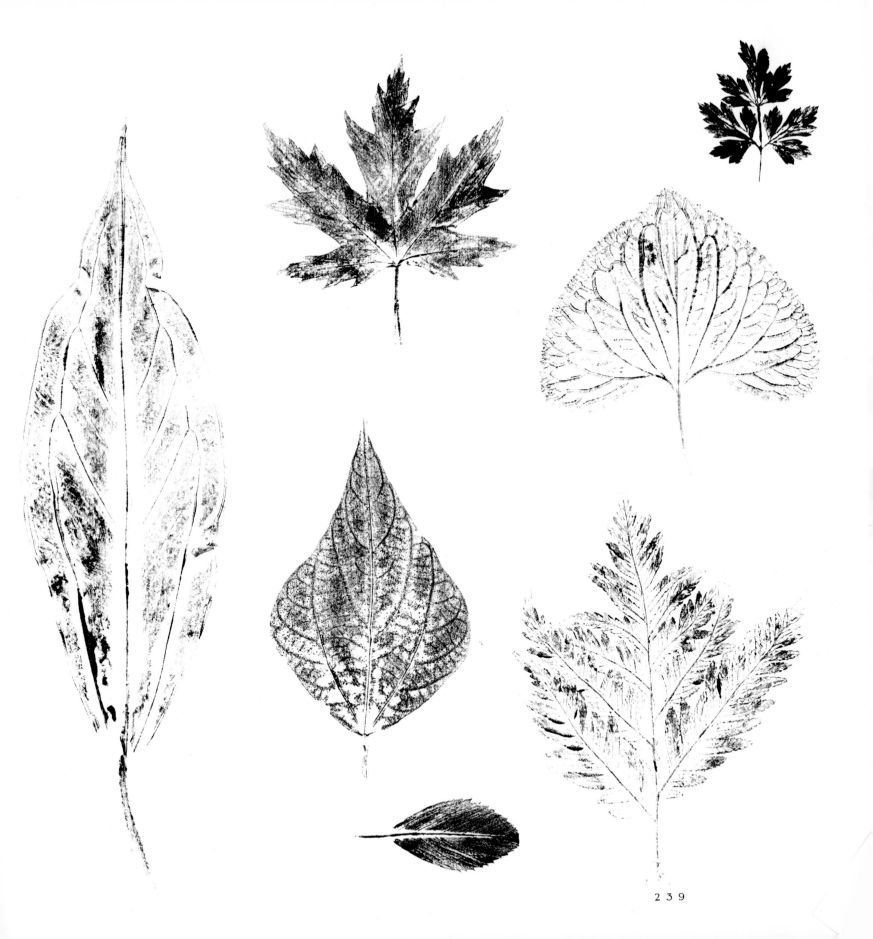

239

LEAF VARIATION THROUGH PRINTS

INDEX OF SCIENTIFIC NAMES

GENERAL INDEX